"In this beautifully written yet very [ ], Miller skillfully combines her knowledge of cognitive-behavioral psychology and deeply rooted biblical truth to help the reader not just grow but be transformed. No matter what stage you're in on your spiritual and personal development journey, this book will empower you and challenge you to be more like Jesus. Stephanie's analogies and examples make the content very relatable. It's time for all of us to stop being complacent in our faith and instead reach higher ground with our Lord, and this book will help you do just that."

—Chou Hallegra,
MA, BCCC, CFTP, CGSC
Founder of Grace & Hope Consulting, LLC

"Stephanie Miller's book, *The Butterfly Blueprint: How to Renew Your Mind and Grow Your Faith*, is the perfect combination of personal stories and sound biblical teaching. She shares from her own experiences and backs up every instance with scripture. This book will suck you in, make you think on a deeper level, and move you to action to seek out a deeper and more profound relationship with Christ. I highly recommend this book to anyone looking for a real-life testimony of growing and walking with Christ through every aspect of life. Stephanie's story, which intricately weaves with scripture and parallels the example of a butterfly egg emerging into a beautiful butterfly, will bless your mind, spirit, and soul."

—Elizabeth Clamon,
CEO/Founder of The Clamon Group and Relentless Hearts Ministries,
Professional Speaker, International Best-Selling Author,
Business Coach, www.ElizabethClamon.com

"With God's Word as her foundation, Stephanie Miller parallels our spiritual renewing with a butterfly in a very personal way. This book will guide you through spiritual transformation from birth, growth, and difficult seasons to a new creation formed by God's hand."

—Stefani Stoltzfus,
Author, Founder of the Warrior Hearted Moms Community

"In a beautiful and easy-to-understand way, *The Butterfly Blueprint: How to Renew Your Mind and Grow Your Faith* shows how the four stages in the life of a butterfly resemble the stages of growth in a Christian's life. This book reminds me of the parables of Jesus. Stephanie Miller uses the familiar elements of creation to explain spiritual truths. She maps out the processes we must all go through to become mature, resemble Jesus in our behavior, and have a heart like His. Yet there's more. *The Butterfly Blueprint* not only gives a plan for growth but also contains a record of Stephanie's personal experiences as she applies the blueprint in her own life. She is a teacher and counselor with integrity for she lives according to the blueprint she designed. I highly recommend this book to anyone who wants to grow into the "butterfly" God designed them to be. It is a reference I will keep for myself and give to others."

—Jane Ault,
Author of *Emotional Freedom: The Choices We Must Make,*
Blogger

THE
Butterfly
BLUEPRINT

How to Renew Your Mind and Grow Your Faith

Stephanie Miller

LUCIDBOOKS

The Butterfly Blueprint
How to Renew Your Mind and Grow Your Faith

ISBN: 978-1-63296-998-9
eISBN: 978-1-63296-388-8

Table of Contents

Introduction   1

The Butterfly Egg   5

Chapter 1   In the Beginning There Was an . . . Egg   7

The Caterpillar   23

Chapter 2   The Hungry Caterpillar: How Do You Eat an Apple?   25

Chapter 3   Growing in Our Awareness   33

Chapter 4   Accepting Yourself as a Caterpillar . . . Temporarily   41

Chapter 5   The Label Maker   47

Inside the Cocoon   53

Chapter 6   Being Authentic about Your Struggle   55

Chapter 7   Your Authentic Story: Butterfly Emerging   65

The Butterfly   75

Chapter 8   The Butterfly Has Emerged, So Now What?   77

Chapter 9   The Purpose of the Butterfly   93

Chapter 10   The Cycle Begins Again   103

Conclusion: The Butterfly in Action   107

Chapter 11   The SMART Goal   109

Chapter 12   Your Step-by-Step Guide to Becoming a Butterfly   121

Chapter 13   Butterfly Declaration   125

Resources   133

Scripture References for Each Chapter   137

Acknowledgments   155

Introduction

*I am convinced that life is 10% what happens to me
and 90% how I react to it.*

—Charles Swindoll

Perspective. Life is all about perspective. We hear all the time that perspective shapes our reality, but I believe our perspective *is* our reality; we know no other reality than this. We are subject to how our personal biases, beliefs, and emotions influence our perceptions.

In graduate school, I worked under a very well-known cognitive psychologist for my thesis. As a graduate student, I had the opportunity to learn more about cognitive psychology, the study of how our thoughts are influenced by many things and how our thoughts lead to our behaviors and actions.

The argument could be this: Do we have a choice when it comes to our reactions or responses, or are they things that happen spontaneously that we cannot influence? You may have heard it said that two people can be in the same scenario, and their reactions could be completely different.

For example, say you are on your way to work when you get a flat tire on a rainy day. Obviously, this isn't ideal, but it also isn't the end of the world for most people.

Person A may respond by laughing and saying something like this: At least it's not storming—I didn't want to go to work anyway.

Person B may respond by yelling, screaming, crying, and saying something like this: Now I'm going to get fired since I can't go to work. This rain is going to ruin my outfit.

Obviously, there's some exaggeration here, but I think you get the point—same situation, different reactions and responses. What influences our reactions and responses? Can we learn to change them? How can we start to live out better responses?

Up to this point, I've talked about psychology, science, and perspective in terms of cognitive-behavioral applications (don't worry, I'll explain more about this later). I want to now shift our focus to a different perspective.

You may have picked up this book for many different reasons. Maybe you know me personally and want to support me. Maybe someone recommended this to you, and you are checking it out. Maybe you are longing for a deeper connection with God and have noticed that you have become stagnant—dare I say lukewarm—in your faith. Maybe you don't have a relationship with God and are thinking something is missing. This spiritual growth and transformation may sound too good to be true, but you might be willing to give it a shot.

Well, you're in luck. The shift in perspective that takes your response from negative to positive, from yelling to smiling, and from worry to peace is simple: *It's your relationship with God.* It is really that easy and yet that hard at the same time. (Please note that while there are many takes on what spiritual growth is, this book refers specifically to Christian spiritual growth unless otherwise stated.)

As your relationship with God becomes the lens through which you view your life, the events that happen seemingly become less critical in determining your future. Life looks different because it is—because you are different. You are no longer tossed to and fro.

We have this hope as an anchor for the soul, firm and secure.

—Heb. 6:19

Looking at life from a heavenly perspective instead of a worldly one is what takes the pressure off yourself and allows you to be who God called you to be. You can live in that freedom.

Freedom. Isn't that what we all want—freedom from worry, fear, loneliness, and rejection? As a personal and spiritual growth coach, I've helped many women obtain this freedom by showing them five key principles for spiritual growth. When they have applied these keys to their lives, they have experienced growth they never thought possible. One of my mentors once told me something like this: *You only know what you know, which means you don't know what you don't know.* There is a whole other side to whatever you're thinking about. These principles have the power to change your life. Yes, I know that is a big statement, and I stand behind it.

But you must be willing to put in the work. The contents of this book shouldn't be something you read and say, "Well, that's nice in theory, but I have no desire to apply it in my own life." Again, I'm going to talk more about what is required from us for lasting change, but know that this message—this personal testimony and story that I share in this book—is not for my own glory; I give all glory to God. It is only through the power of His Spirit alive in me that I can share this truth.

As you go through this book, you will notice scriptures throughout. They are also listed by chapter at the end of the book. Journaling and Food for Thought questions are located at the end of some of the chapters, which gives you a chance to reflect on the main points of the chapter. This book will be equally valuable to you whether you read it by yourself or in a group. As you start to see my message (really God's message since He is speaking through me), I encourage you to start to consider what your message from Him might be. What may God want to use in your life in order to help others? What have you overcome or are walking through that you think someone else going through the same thing should know?

This book is structured according to the stages of a butterfly. We start with the butterfly egg and end by discussing the butterfly as the result of the transformation that takes place inside the cocoon. The first part of the book discusses from the butterfly perspective each stage in terms of general faith and new creation in Christ. The second part of the book challenges you to apply these same terms to other specific areas of your life and asks you to examine these areas and ask yourself, "What stage am I currently in? What do I need in order to move to the next stage?"

While this book is about spiritual growth and transformation from a butterfly perspective, it is more than that. It is my personal obedience to God. It is my life out there for all to see. It is a call for you to show that same courage and obedience by working each of these areas of your life and being open to what God wants to do in you, with you, and through you.

The worst thing we could ever do is read the Bible and not apply it to our lives. I'm not saying that this book is like the Bible, but I am saying that if you hope to change or see any change in your life, you must be willing to put in the work and apply these principles to your life.

One of my favorite authors, Lysa TerKeurst, said, "Inspiration and information without personal application will never amount to transformation."[1]

You can finally take God out of that box once and for all and let Him have His way in your heart.

This is what life is about—reading, learning, applying, and growing. In the next section of the book, we explore the tools necessary for spiritual growth—from an egg, caterpillar, cocoon, and butterfly standpoint. These tools can (and should) be applied to any area of your life. When applied with a renewed mind and open heart, there is no telling what can happen. With practice, patience, and willingness, spiritual growth is possible in every area of your life. You can finally take God out of that box once and for all and let Him have His way in your heart. You can finally emerge from the cocoon, spread your God-given wings, and fly.

---

1. Lyza TerKeurst, *Uninvited*, Google Books, 23.

THE
Butterfly
EGG

We begin our journey into the butterfly perspective by first looking at the butterfly egg. Adult butterflies lay eggs very systematically and intentionally on various leaves. In fact, that is the main job of an adult butterfly—to lay eggs before dying since the lifespan of adult butterflies is rather short. The color, shape, and texture of the eggs are all different, depending on the species of the butterfly. And just like human eggs, each butterfly egg is unique and different. There are no two butterfly eggs that have the same DNA. Some types of eggs are more transparent than others, so if you look closely, you can actually see the caterpillar start to develop. Just like this developing creature, we have been created by God for a purpose.

As we begin looking at our spiritual growth through the life cycle of the butterfly, we must start with the potential of the caterpillar inside the egg. Each stage in the butterfly's life cycle has a purpose and a goal, and the egg stage is representative of our potential and purpose in Christ. The goal in this stage is to successfully avoid getting eaten or destroyed and then hatch from the egg. The goal for us in this stage is to be open to a new way of thinking about ourselves, our spiritual growth, and our relationship with Jesus. Just as the butterfly eggs sit on the leaf waiting to hatch, we, too, sit and wait for change to begin. Are you as ready as I am? Let's get started by looking at transformation versus spiritual growth. What comes first? Does it matter? What role do we play in each?

CHAPTER 1

In the Beginning There Was an ... Egg

Which came first, the chicken or the egg?

I've never understood why the order of the chicken and the egg is important. But regardless of whether you think the chicken or the egg came first, both exist together. In order to get the egg, you need the chicken, but just because you have the chicken doesn't mean you automatically get the egg. In order to get an egg from the chicken, there are choices to make and then steps to take. This is the same with spiritual growth and transformation. When we are saved, we receive salvation. Salvation is the forgiveness of our sins that we receive by accepting Jesus Christ as our Lord and Savior (John 3:16–17). We also experience a transformation as the Holy Spirit deposits Himself in us and the process of sanctification begins (Eph. 1:13–14).

For God so loved the world that he gave his one and only Son, that whoever believes in him shall not perish but have eternal life. For God did not send his Son into the world to condemn the world, but to save the world through him.

—John 3:16–17

And you also were included in Christ when you heard the message of truth, the gospel of your salvation. When you believed, you were marked in him with a seal, the promised Holy Spirit, who is a deposit guaranteeing our inheritance until the redemption of those who are God's possession—to the praise of his glory.

—Eph. 1:13–14

Sanctification is the process of becoming holy. This process is something that takes time and does not happen automatically; instead, it requires action and effort on our part. Has the butterfly always been a butterfly, or did it transform into a butterfly from something else? Before it was a caterpillar, what was it? We know the answer—before it was a caterpillar, it was an egg. The egg contains the cells that are needed for growth into a caterpillar first and then transformation into a butterfly.

Our lives are much the same. We start as a collection of cells in our mother's womb, and those cells form our limbs, brains, and other vital organs needed to sustain life. After we have grown and developed inside the womb, we mature enough to enter this world. Once the cells of the egg have properly formed the caterpillar, it is ready to hatch and begin the second stage of life.

Yet you brought me out of the womb;
   you made me trust in you, even at my mother's breast.
From birth I was cast on you;
   from my mother's womb you have been my God.

—Ps. 22:9–10

From our births, we are innately human, and it isn't until we accept Jesus Christ into our hearts as our Lord and Savior that our rebirth begins.

What if we parallel a caterpillar-butterfly with someone who is, as scripture says of those who don't know God, dead in their sins (Eph. 2:1–5) and someone who is transformed into a new creation in Christ?

> *As for you, you were dead in your transgressions and sins, in which you used to live when you followed the ways of this world and of the ruler of the kingdom of the air, the spirit who is now at work in those who are disobedient. All of us also lived among them at one time, gratifying the cravings of our flesh and following its desires and thoughts. Like the rest, we were by nature deserving of wrath. But because of his great love for us, God, who is rich in mercy, made us alive with Christ even when we were dead in transgressions—it is by grace you have been saved.*
>
> —Eph. 2:1–5

> *Therefore, if anyone is in Christ, the new creation has come: The old has gone, the new is here!*
>
> —2 Cor. 5:17

The interesting thing about a caterpillar is that since it can only crawl on the ground, it has a very limited viewpoint of the world around it. It only sees what is in front of it. On the other hand, the butterfly barely resembles the caterpillar when it emerges from the cocoon. Its viewpoint is no longer confined to the ground; instead, it can fly with its wings and see the world in a whole new way. But what would happen if that butterfly didn't act like a butterfly? What would happen if it never tried to fly and instead tried to scoot around on the ground, just like it did when it was a caterpillar? What is the difference between believing, knowing, growing, and using its wings?

The answer is Jesus—the change that happens in response to the Holy Spirit being deposited in your body. Yes, the initial change occurred—the caterpillar turning into a butterfly—but what if it stopped there? What if the butterfly, even though equipped with wings, never tried to fly? As a result of doubt and fear, the butterfly might drag itself on the ground like it is still a caterpillar. This is what we are like until we accept Jesus Christ as Lord and Savior. It is what so many of us can fall victim to if we're not careful. It's *wasted potential.* There is so much God wants to do for us, but He won't force Himself into our lives. It is only when we make that decision for ourselves that true and lasting transformation and growth begin. We reach what I call our "hatching point."

When you are given new life through the grace of God and He transforms you into a new creation, you cannot just sit on it and do nothing. We can't afford to become stagnant or complacent in our faith. You only have to feel that way a short time to be convinced that you are a caterpillar and that's all you'll ever be. If you aren't constantly working on your faith and relationship with God, then you will limit your own choices by your own thinking.

I know the wasted potential part all too well as it was one of the key markers in my testimony when I first came to Christ. As you read my extremely raw and vulnerable story scattered throughout this book, I encourage you to identify when I was still acting like a caterpillar and how I started to act like a butterfly. Identifying stages of spiritual growth in my life may help you identify where you are in your own life.

We aren't transformed into new creations to simply just be; there is a reason, there is a cause, and there is a purpose. God is a God of reconciliation and redemption, and there is nothing from your past that He does not forgive or redeem in some way.

Transformation is a call to action; hatching is a call to action.

An example of this comes from the book of Acts when Paul, formerly known as Saul, has an encounter with Jesus, who changes his life forever.

As he neared Damascus on his journey, suddenly a light from heaven flashed around him. He fell to the ground and heard a voice say to him, "Saul, Saul, why do you persecute me?"

"Who are you, Lord?" Saul asked.

"I am Jesus, whom you are persecuting," he replied. "Now get up and go into the city, and you will be told what you must do."

The men traveling with Saul stood there speechless; they heard the sound but did not see anyone. Saul got up from the ground, but when he opened his eyes, he could see nothing. So they led him by the hand into Damascus. For three days he was blind, and did not eat or drink anything.

In Damascus there was a disciple named Ananias. The Lord called to him in a vision, "Ananias!"

"Yes, Lord," he answered.

The Lord told him, "Go to the house of Judas on Straight Street and ask for a man from Tarsus named Saul, for he is praying. In a vision he has seen a man named Ananias come and place his hands on him to restore his sight."

"Lord," Ananias answered, "I have heard many reports about this man and all the harm he has done to your holy people in Jerusalem. And he has come here with authority from the chief priests to arrest all who call on your name."

But the Lord said to Ananias, "Go! This man is my chosen instrument to proclaim my name to the Gentiles and their kings and to the people of Israel. I will show him how much he must suffer for my name."

Then Ananias went to the house and entered it. Placing his hands on Saul, he said, "Brother Saul, the Lord—Jesus, who appeared to you on the road as you were coming here—has sent me so that you may see again and be filled with the Holy Spirit." Immediately, something like scales fell from Saul's eyes, and he could see again. He got up and was baptized, and after taking some food, he regained his strength.

—Acts 9:3–19

What strikes me is that when Jesus asks Saul why he is persecuting Him, Saul responds, "Who are you, Lord?" (Acts 9:5). There is an openness and receptive spirit about this answer because Jesus could have ignored the question or said something far worse. Much like us, Saul didn't know he was searching until he found what he had been missing.

Let me back up. What made you decide to commit your life to Christ? Maybe you grew up a Christian, and it's all you've ever known. Maybe you needed to figure out and explore what else life was about before making a commitment to Christ, or maybe you still don't know whether you believe any of this, and that's okay. If we look at the story of the Apostle Paul, we see that a willingness and heart readiness is all he really needed to be transformed. The hatching point of our new Christian life is just the acceptance of what it means to be not only a follower but also a lover of Jesus. It can come suddenly when you least expect it, or it can be a stirring inside you that has been going on for some time. However you experience it, it's just like an egg hatching—it literally breaks you.

It's true that you don't know what you have until it's gone, but it is also true that you don't know what you are missing until it arrives. In my own life, I was at a point of hopelessness and despair before I opened my heart to the possibility that God loves me and has a special purpose for my life. I thought life was fine before Christ. I felt empty, like something was missing, but it wasn't anything I couldn't temporarily stuff away or distract myself from thinking about.

I'll never forget the night I officially said yes to God and invited Him to transform my heart from the inside out. I was at a big outdoor Christian music festival with a guy I'd had a crush on all summer. He was a coworker who seemed different from any other guy I had ever met, and that difference was appealing to me. One night he invited me to a concert where I learned his secret.

As the band Skillet finished their set on stage and the next performer came on, a hush came over the crowd. The mood of the crowd shifted. Everyone in that audience switched from having a good time and rocking out to really worshipping and humbling themselves as Chris Tomlin performed. I remember looking around and seeing people singing with their arms raised, tears streaming down their faces. For a moment I felt like an outsider, like I didn't belong there. I couldn't be one of these people because I was nothing like them. I turned to walk away when suddenly Chris Tomlin began talking about where his life was before Jesus. He said that no matter what mess you are in or what you did in the past, Christ could save you and give you new life.

New life, I thought and almost scoffed. *That's a tall promise, but I'm desperate for another way. I'm tired of my life now, and I believe there is something more.* So I closed my eyes and said the prayer that Chris invited us to say, repenting of my sins and inviting Jesus in my heart to change me into the person I was created to be. My heart was open, and I was ready for change, but it proved harder than I imagined to give up the old me and start living as the new me.

Pursuing Jesus and living out His purpose requires dedication, discipline, and diligence. Paul talks about this struggle between flesh and spirit.

For the flesh desires what is contrary to the Spirit, and the Spirit what is contrary to the flesh. They are in conflict with each other, so that you are not to do whatever you want.

—Gal. 5:17

He even talks later about the struggle we experience between wanting to do good and actually doing good. The saying "old habits die hard" definitely comes to mind here.

I do not understand what I do. For what I want to do I do not do, but what I hate I do.

—Rom. 7:15

Our old life doesn't just go away, so that means our friends and lifestyles don't just change by themselves. Your party-girl reputation doesn't dissolve, and the endless temptations to fall back into the parties, the alcohol, and the bad decisions don't completely disappear, but in time and with practice, your old way of living can become less appealing, and making decisions that encourage a stronger relationship with God starts to become easier. Part of what is to blame is how we listen to and respond to our hearts. Society tells us to listen to our hearts and go with what they tell us, but scripture paints a much different picture.

The truth about the heart is somewhat contradicting. While God gives you "the desires of your heart" (Ps. 37:4), scripture also tells us that "the heart is deceitful above all things" (Jer. 17:9). So do our hearts' desires always get answered, or are we to ignore what our hearts tell us because they cannot be trusted?

Take delight in the LORD,
* and he will give you the desires of your heart.*

—Ps. 37:4

The heart is deceitful above all things and beyond cure.
* Who can understand it?*

—Jer. 17:9

Understanding the condition of our heart is the first step in determining heart readiness. The desires of your heart reflect those that are both of this world and of God. Just because you have a deep desire in your heart does not mean it will come true, but it does serve a purpose. The goal is to discern what your own personal desires are from what God is placing in your heart to have you fulfill.

With my second child, I was determined to have a VBAC (vaginal birth after cesarean). I did my research, hired a doula to answer some questions, and was prepared to be my own advocate at the hospital when the time came. My son had a two-vessel cord in utero, and I was advised that I shouldn't go past 39 weeks. I had scheduled a tentative induction date at around 39 weeks. I wasn't too excited about having to be induced and trying for a VBAC if he didn't come by then, but I was trusting God that I would go into labor on my own before the induction date.

At my 38-week appointment, my midwife checked me, and I was 70 percent effaced and about 3.5 centimeters dilated. I was ecstatic as she did a membrane sweep and told me I should be going into labor naturally in a few days. I wouldn't need to worry about the scheduled induction the following week. Two days later, my water broke, but my labor never started. I waited at my house for labor to start, but after 18 hours, I decided I should go in just in case there was a chance of getting an infection.

I could go into lengthy detail here about the process and the choice I made, but ultimately, as much as I had planned and prepared for my VBAC, it didn't happen. I didn't even try for it and opted for a repeat cesarean section instead. I struggle with this decision still because I wanted to do what was best for my baby and myself, and I thought that going for a VBAC would redeem the birth experience I'd had with my daughter. The desire of my heart was focused entirely on having a successful VBAC. Even though I didn't get that, I did get the desire of my heart by having a beautiful baby boy and, to my surprise, a much easier recovery. God did redeem my previous birth experience, just not in the way I expected Him to.

Many are the plans in a person's heart,
 but it is the LORD's purpose that prevails.

—Prov. 19:21

I share this story to remind you that sometimes our desires are not our true desires, and we need to be able to understand what our desired outcomes or ideas really symbolize. In my example, I thought a VBAC was the answer, but my hope and trust in God to deliver my baby safe and sound was what my heart truly longed for. Despite having to give up the picture-perfect VBAC in my mind, God still revealed to me the true desire of my heart, and from my willingness to veer off course and go against my perfectly laid out plan, He was faithful to provide me with my sweet baby boy.

While this story can demonstrate so many things about God's goodness, mercy, and grace (in addition to showing that He is a redeemer of all things), I also believe it provides an example of the true desires of our heart—what happens when the desires placed in us by the world lead us astray and what happens when we are in tune with our desires directed by God.

One way to determine what a worldly desire of the heart might be instead of a godly desire is to pray. David in Psalm 139 provides a moving prayer that not only asks God to reveal the sin in his heart but to also show him the better way. Humility is always important when discussing change and transformation.

Search me, God, and know my heart;
 test me and know my anxious thoughts.
See if there is any offensive way in me,
 and lead me in the way everlasting.

—Ps. 139:23–24

Don't get me wrong, as much as I love sacred prayer with my heavenly Father, I still sometimes wish there was a magic answer, a checklist, or even a flowchart to lead me to the correct answer. Honestly, though, if we could go to these things to find the answer, we wouldn't need God. He cleverly designed us to need Him, so the best thing to do is sit down and have an honest and open conversation with God about the condition of your heart. If you don't know what the condition of your heart is, a great first step is to ask God to reveal it to you, and He will. This isn't a one-and-done thing; rather, it takes us consistently checking in with our heart motives and having an honest dialogue with God to reach this.

Constant heart cleanup, as I call it, takes some time and effort on our part. We have to be willing to ask ourselves hard questions and be okay when God reveals the answer. One important thing to remember is that once we receive salvation (being right with God), we start the process of sanctification (being set apart or made holy). But the process of purifying our hearts to live more like Jesus only goes as far as we're willing to go and let go. That means that you and I have a crucial role in our spiritual growth.

Wouldn't it be nice if once we received salvation, we could sit back and relax and let Jesus do all the work? Wouldn't it be nice if once we were saved and promised eternal life through our belief in Jesus, our former demons would never haunt us again? I wish I could tell you that all our struggles and issues magically disappear, but that isn't the case. We must constantly work on our caterpillar mindset—our worldly thoughts, selfish motives, and sinful desires. A caterpillar settles into a routine and gets used to thinking and doing things its own way, convinced that while its life isn't anything special, it isn't terrible, either.

But Christ didn't come to give us an okay, fine, or even good life. Christ came to give us an *abundant* and *full* life, and out of that abundance come the things you never ever imagined before.

I have come that they may have life, and have it to the full.
—John 10:10

17

The first part of that verse says that the enemy comes to "steal and kill and destroy." And boy, does he ever! He wants to take you out of the game before you are even in it, which is often reflected by trying to lure you back into your old ways. That is important to remember when determining what steps we need to take to become more like Christ. The choice to turn away from sin entirely and toward God may be easier for some of us than for others. So how do we maintain that momentum or that passion after the initial wonder and excitement have worn off?

After I became a Christian in my early 20s, I started dating the guy who had introduced me to Christ. At first, it was easy and so great to be someone I had never been before and live a completely different way. But it wasn't long before my old habits and struggles started to creep back in, and when our relationship ended, so did my active pursuit of Christ. It was easier to sink back into my old ways than to continue to navigate this new Christian identity, especially after losing the crutch of my then-boyfriend who had played a huge role in my salvation. Instead, I started going to parties and drinking again, slowly pushing God out of my life by making decisions contrary to those of a Christian woman.

I missed two important ingredients that are needed to maintain our faith and commitment and be an active follower of Jesus. The first is to be a living example for others by not conforming to the wonders of the world but instead having a renewed mind, and the second is to be in this world and not of this world.

Once we accept salvation, we are in the process of being sanctified—set apart—but it is up to us to seek God and ask Him what we are being set apart for, to be able to understand and live out the calling that we are to be in the world and not of the world (John 17:15–18), and that we need to have a renewed mind (Rom. 12:2). I discuss this in the next chapter.

My prayer is not that you take them out of the world but that you protect them from the evil one. They are not of the world, even as I am not of it. Sanctify them by the

*truth; your word is truth. As you sent me into the world,
I have sent them into the world.*

—John 17:15–18

Jesus was no stranger to being around people, places, or things of this world. He spoke openly to certain women that everyone else looked down on and even had dinner with a tax collector. He put Himself around all sorts of people and led by example. He didn't shy away from the hard places or the hard people but actually proceeded to do quite the opposite.

*When the teachers of the law who were Pharisees saw him
eating with the sinners and tax collectors, they asked his
disciples: "Why does He eat with tax collectors and sinners?"
On hearing this, Jesus told them, "It is not the healthy
who need a doctor, but the sick. I have not come to call the
righteous, but sinners."*

—Mark 2:16–17

If Jesus never went to these types of places and engaged with these types of people, there is no telling where you or I would be now. The world as we know it would be very different. We can be thankful that Jesus meets us right where we are, even when that is a lonely, worldly place. There is no place on earth He won't go to find us, and we can be confident that in Him, we are no longer slaves to our worldly ways, but we are free.

*But thanks be to God that, though you used to be slaves
to sin, you have come to obey from your heart the pattern
of teaching that has now claimed your allegiance. You
have been set free from sin and have become slaves to
righteousness.*

—Rom. 6:17–18

Do not conform to the pattern of this world, but be transformed by the renewing of your mind. Then you will be able to test and approve what God's will is—his good, pleasing and perfect will.

—Rom. 12:2

From this freedom we experience in Christ comes our response by renewing our minds. Some of us may have been told there are certain things we are expected to do that renew our minds. We have to read the Bible. We have to go to church. We have to pray. We have to try to be good people. Saying you have to do something is like saying you need to do something. Both imply discontentment and that you measure your worth or value conditionally (based on whether you did what you said you needed to do). A renewed mind focuses on understanding your reasoning for doing things and making sure you are not just following the crowd.

Why do these things in the first place? What is your motivation behind being good?

I recently asked these questions to a Bible study group I was facilitating, and some of their answers surprised me. Many of the ladies said they do all these things because they fear going to hell or becoming a nasty person. It was quite startling to hear that many people obey God or seek to obey Him out of fear of punishment and what may happen if they choose not to do so.

Take little children, for instance, those around the ages of three or four. For the most part, how do they behave toward you? How do they respond to the things you ask them to do, or do they ever do something without your telling them to? Why do you think they do those things?

A renewed mind focuses on understanding your reasoning for doing things and making sure you are not just following the crowd.

Do you think they are afraid you won't love them anymore if they don't obey, or do they desire to please you with their actions?

Personally, I think most kids want to please their parents and make them happy, so they are motivated to follow the rules out of love and not fear. Of course, this is largely dependent on the type of parent we are, and God is our ultimate example of a loving parent.

> *There is no fear in love. But perfect love drives out fear, because fear has to do with punishment. The one who fears is not made perfect in love.*
>
> —1 John 4:18

Our renewed mind must desire to be transformed by having an obedient heart out of love, not fear, for the Father. When you remember that there is nothing you can do to separate yourself from God, no way that He will ever stop pursuing you, it gets a little easier to be motivated to change out of love and not fear.

> *For I am convinced that neither death nor life, neither angels nor demons, neither the present nor the future, nor any powers, neither height nor depth, nor anything else in all creation, will be able to separate us from the love of God that is in Christ Jesus our Lord.*
>
> —Rom. 8:38–39

Even though we always have God's love to fall back on, many of us still choose to stay right where we are and never leave our comfort zones. We either stay an egg that never hatches or busy caterpillars that are just going through the motions of life. What happens when we stay right where we are and are afraid to grow beyond what we are used to?

In life, you can have comfort and growth but not both at the same time.

Interestingly, we don't often think of being comfortable as necessarily a bad thing (hello, yoga pants). But when it comes to our spiritual growth and our pursuit of Jesus, we can be too comfortable and settle into a rut of complacent faith and stagnant growth.

Growth only happens outside our comfort zones.

There is a unique thing that happens as caterpillars grow; their skins don't grow with them. Instead of growing into their bodies, they shed their exoskeletons and take on new skin and a new body. If we think in terms of a caterpillar, when our jeans become too tight and our shirts too small, it's time to size up and step out. Life is constant change, so if we neglect to embrace this, we will inevitably stay stuck and uncomfortable because who likes to wear pants that are too small?

Food for Thought Questions:

- Describe your hatching point. What steps have you taken or plan to take to reach your hatching point?
- Describe your comfort zone. What about it makes it safe? What would stepping out of your comfort zone look like?
- How might you know if you are successfully pursuing growth instead of comfort?
- Read Mark 4, the parable of the seed. What does Jesus say the different types of soil represent? How can we keep from becoming like the seed that doesn't grow? Can you identify any instances in your own life where either you or another person responded to the Word of God in any of the ways Jesus describes?

In the next few chapters, we will start to look at spiritual growth separate from transformation. We will look at it as a step-by-step way to grow a deeper relationship with God. Once you've hatched into a caterpillar, you really have two choices: feast on what is good or feast on what is bad as you prepare to enter the cocoon. Let's discuss what happens when you choose each one.

THE
Caterpillar

Once the caterpillar hatches from the egg (a new life as a Christian), it is tasked with the responsibility to eat as much as it can from the leaf it hatched on. It does this so it can be big enough and ready to enter the cocoon as part of the transformation. However, before we jump to that vantage point, it is important to compare the different perspectives butterflies and caterpillars have based on where they are and what they can see relative to their locations.

CHAPTER 2

The Hungry Caterpillar: How Do You Eat an Apple?

Have you read or are you familiar with the book *The Very Hungry Caterpillar* by Eric Carle? In the book, a caterpillar hatches from an egg on a leaf and then proceeds to eat several food items for a week before chewing through the leaf it was on and settling into a cocoon to complete its transformation into a butterfly. The book tells specifically of the many random foods (Swiss cheese, salami, and cupcakes, to name a few) the caterpillar eats through and gets a stomachache as a result of eating too much too fast.

What Happens When We Eat Too Much Too Fast?

Let's say I give you your favorite apple. Maybe it's a Honey Crisp, a Gala, a Golden Delicious, or, my personal favorite, a Granny Smith. How would you eat it? Would you attempt to put the whole thing in your mouth, core and all? Or would you start to take small bites of the apple?

How would you take the bites? Would you take all different sized bites or try to keep biting pieces of the apple without fully chewing and swallowing the previous bite first? Or would you take random bites at the top, middle, and bottom of the apple, making you unsure where you already took a bite or making you miss part of the apple? Perhaps you might take a more meticulous approach, maybe biting around the perimeter of the apple and then the top and bottom so you can be sure you don't miss any of the deliciousness.

When we eat too much too fast, we can't enjoy it or absorb it properly. Not only should we be careful about how fast we eat, but we should be mindful of what we eat. A rich, chocolatey dessert is not something we can eat all at once. In order to get the most out of our experience, we need to eat slowly and take our time. The same principle can apply to other things.

Taking small, manageable bites and meticulous bites in an ordered fashion is no different than what it takes to grow spiritually. If you try to fit the whole apple in your mouth at once, it is going to be impossible and probably painful. Therefore, if you take small bites and finish the first bite before moving on to the next, it is easier and even enjoyable to eat the apple (even if you would rather have that rich chocolate cake).

That is how we should approach spiritual growth and reading and understanding the Word of God. We take small, manageable steps (or bites) that are enjoyable in such a way that we can visibly see our progress. We don't try to make too many changes at once because we know that is both overwhelming and unsustainable. When it is time for us to feed ourselves, it is better to digest slowly than to inhale our spiritual nourishment. We need to read and accept truths bit-by-bit sometimes instead of all at once, especially if we are hoping for lasting change.

"The mind feasts on what it focuses on,"[2] a quote from Lysa TerKeurst, demonstrates that we need to be careful what we are feeding our minds. We will have a different outlook based on what we fill ourselves up with. For example, if I only read beauty magazines that talk about what beauty is in terms of a size four, blonde-haired, blue-eyed, gorgeous, tan woman with perfectly straight and white teeth, then I'm

---

2. Lysa TerKeurst, *Uninvited*, 23.

very likely going to feel like I don't measure up. On the other hand, if I fill myself with the truths of who I am in Christ and what it means to be beautiful in the eyes of our heavenly Father, I am going to understand and appreciate all that it means to be a daughter of the King.

As caterpillars, we think of things from our own perspectives; we can only see what we can see and don't know any different. We also fill ourselves with what the world says is the right way as a means of having control over our lives. As butterflies, however, we take inventory of our own perspectives and are open to the possibility that there are things in this world that we will not know or ever understand, much less have control over; we have faith in God and His plan. This is all part of the spiritual growth process we undergo once we receive salvation.

What does spiritual growth mean to you?

I know. It means growing spiritually. (Nice try!) But what does that *look* like?

Growing closer to God.

Having a deeper relationship with God.

Reading the Bible more.

Praying more.

Feeling more in tune with the Holy Spirit.

These are all good answers, but I want to challenge you to think bigger, think broader.

We (as Christians) sometimes tend to compartmentalize our faith or relationship with God. This limited thinking is demonstrated in the areas of life we have not surrendered. The most obvious example of this is being all about Jesus on Sunday while you attend church, meanwhile doing whatever else you want during the week, even things that are contrary to someone who loves Jesus. Early in my faith journey, I was one of those people who attended church on Sunday, acting one way but completely acting against everything the Bible talks about the second I exited those doors. I could turn it off and on in the blink of an eye, and I knew when to play Jesus girl. The idea that we can act so differently from one situation to the next and compartmentalize our faith shows our lack of letting God be God. Instead, we are content to interact with God only when it's easy and convenient for us. *Ouch!*

Some of us are aware of this disconnect, yet we do nothing about it. Then there are others of us who don't realize that we put God in a box and limit where we see Him in our lives. We have special moments or times during the day or week when we talk to God, but we don't look to Him as always being with us.

This mindset can be dangerous, especially as it relates to spiritual growth and our ability to look beyond our caterpillar stage. Operating in the belief that God can only be God when you are doing the obvious God-things severely limits your growth and potential to make a Kingdom impact.

God is so much bigger than just helping you read the Bible or allowing you to enjoy worship music during church. What would it look like to see God in other areas of your life? You see Him as you seek to develop a deeper relationship with Him, but what if that relationship with Him expanded into *every* area of your life?

What would it look like to grow spiritually in your marriage?

What would it look like to grow spiritually in your career?

What would it look like to grow spiritually in your finances?

What would it look like to grow spiritually in your health?

Spiritual growth is any area of your life that you allow God into. Friends, we serve a big God—a huge God, a God who is bigger and better than we can comprehend. The truth is, He yearns to operate in all these other areas of our lives. But as big and bold as He is, He is also a gentleman. God is not going to bang down the door of our hearts; instead, He will knock softly and wait patiently for the invitation to grow us and transform us in those areas. Some of us are able to see this and extend Him the invitation, while others of us go our whole lives

---

Spiritual growth is any area of your life that you allow God into.

---

without allowing Him to impact those areas of our lives. The special thing about the butterfly perspective as it pertains to spiritual growth and transformation is that it isn't an all-or-nothing thing. You aren't either a caterpillar or a butterfly; instead, you can be at different stages in different areas of your life. You will have an opportunity to take an inventory at the back of this book with some questions to help you determine what might be hindering your growth in the common areas. After you process your answers, you will be one step closer to making the choices and the mindset shift needed to move into the transformed butterfly God has called you to be.

I'm not going to sugarcoat it; this type of spiritual growth is not easy. The enemy would rather we stay in bondage and darkness. He doesn't want us to allow God to grow us spiritually in every area of our lives. He prefers that we keep God in a box and open that box only when it is easy and convenient for us. He knows that God will only take us as far as we are willing to go, so he continues to tempt us to push God out of every area of our lives.

God knows this. He knows what Satan wants to do and even knows how he wants to do it. God seeks to draw us out of the comfortable and familiar and lead us to the less secure but ultimately more satisfying way of life. Is it easy? *Nope.* Is it automatic? *Not even close.* Is it rewarding and life-altering to grow spiritually in *every* area of your life? Unimaginably *yes.*

From the caterpillar perspective, we are ready to enter the cocoon once we understand that spiritual growth is not limited to just one area of our lives and comes from having a renewed and transformed mind. Without renewed minds, we will always try to stifle God based on our limited understanding. Caterpillars can't fly to see what a butterfly can, so they only see a limited distance from where they are. In our example of where we are in response to seeing God in every area, this implies a limited view and even a limited understanding of God. In this stage, we need to be careful not to overestimate our ability to know what God is doing in our lives. The song "King of the World" by Natalie Grant explains this further, how we tend to limit our understanding of God in our lives based on what we can see and experience.

If we are not careful, just like the song says, our understanding of God is based on the box we put Him in. We try to keep God contained and control the outcomes based on our knowledge and perspective. It is so much easier to trust when we know everything or at least think we do. Friends, control is the enemy of trust.

Don't keep God in a safe box; put him in the sovereign box.

Ouch! I'll admit that I forget this more than I'd like to willingly admit. I know God's got this (any situation in our lives), but sometimes that doesn't stop me from trying to get it also. The greatest difference between a renewed mind and an unrenewed mind is the understanding and appreciation of our limited perspectives. That is why it is so important to have a renewed mind through feasting on the truth found in the Word of God, not just a little bit here and there but completely immersing ourselves in it, which gives us what we need to open up our eyes and be ready to enter our cocoon stage. It is not my job to do everything; what a relief to know I'm not in control but to know the one who is.

Let's recap what we've discussed so far:
- Transformation is the initial acceptance of Christ in your heart as God deposits Himself in you. This initial transformation comes from a decision influenced by a ready and open heart.
- Spiritual growth is the result of the Spirit working in us to show God's hand in *every* area of our lives. Spiritual growth is making choices and taking small steps to ultimately become the person God has created you to be (called sanctification).

- Both require a choice. Both require us to do our part in the process, but you can't have spiritual growth without initial transformation (called salvation).
- When we proclaim Jesus as our Lord and Savior, transformation occurs. When we recognize that we are transformed, our opportunity for spiritual growth begins.

Measuring Out

How do we know whether we are growing spiritually in an area of our life? Are we measuring up to what God has intended for us in each area? What does spiritual growth look like in our finances, marriages, and relationships? It might be better to ask yourself, "Am I measuring out?"

Take your arms and stretch them out to either side or in front of you. What are some activities you do that give you an opportunity to extend your arms?

Hugging. Giving. Touching. Reaching. These are the things we do that involve others. Growing in the different areas of our lives this way is to look out for the interests of others and not for our own selfish gain.

> *Do nothing out of selfish ambition or vain conceit. Rather, in humility value others above yourselves, not looking to your own interests but each of you to the interests of the others.*
>
> —Phil. 2:3–4

When we are able to look at others and place their needs above our own, we are sowing the fruit of the Spirit. One way to measure this is to determine what fruit—visible fruit—we are bearing in that area.

> *But the fruit of the Spirit is love, joy, peace, forbearance, kindness, goodness, faithfulness, gentleness and self-control. Against such things there is no law.*
>
> —Gal. 5:22–23

The fruit of the Spirit is often used to describe several things. Looking at the fruit of the Spirit in terms of spiritual growth, we can examine our thoughts, choices, and actions. Take love, for example. We choose to think kind and gentle thoughts. We choose to practice faithfulness and self-control. The fruit of the Spirit is evidence of the Holy Spirit at work in us.

Examining our thoughts, choices, and actions in every area of life helps give us an idea of the type of fruit we're producing. If you would like to have a list of different areas of life to examine, please refer to the resources section in the back of this book where you will find the Wheel of Life exercise. This exercise will provide you with different areas to self-examine your growth and rate your level of satisfaction in each area. From the rating you give based on a 10-point scale, you can also apply the butterfly perspective as having potential for growth. By looking at it this way, you will have your eyes opened to what may need to happen in order to see God move in that particular area.

"Against such things there is no law" (Gal. 5:23). This leads us directly back to the importance of spiritual transformation as not only how you act on the outside but also how you think on the inside.

Law implies a fear of punishment. Remember, a renewed mind doesn't live from a fear perspective but from a love perspective. This is a choice and requires practice, patience, and willingness to achieve. The good news is that we are neither perfect nor expected to be. The One who is perfect has already paid the price for you and me. Once we understand this, we are no longer trapped in our caterpillar thinking by filling ourselves up with all the junk and garbage the world wants to throw at us. Instead, we put our hope and trust in Christ for our growth by feasting on the truth.

CHAPTER 3

Growing in Our Awareness

Have you ever been out to dinner, finishing up your meal, and the person you are with points out that you have food stuck in your teeth? (Of course, that is after you have been talking and grinning the entire meal.)

What do you do when someone points that out to you? I believe we might respond one of four ways:

A. Smile and say thank you, excuse yourself to the restroom, look at the food in the mirror, and get it out.
B. Smile and say thank you, and try to remove it at the table.
C. Run away mortified.
D. Say you know and did it on purpose just to see if that person would say anything.

Let me just say I am the proud owner of adult braces, so I can really relate to this example. I am most likely to do A, although B would be possible if I had a makeup mirror to look at. And C might happen if I was on an important date. D is interesting because I know no one ever purposely gets food stuck in their teeth. This response is more defensive and deflective.

Either way, once we become aware of the food stuck in our teeth, we do something about it. We don't just start picking our teeth for no reason, and we don't simply ignore the food and hope it goes away. We have to know something is there before we can take steps to get it out. So once we know it's there, we do what is needed to fix the situation.

The process of self-awareness is the same. You become aware of yourself, your likes, dislikes, worries, fears, insecurities, and even worldly crutches by analyzing the world based on behavior and consequences. These very things shape how you view others and how you view yourself. It isn't enough just to know you see the world the way you do; you must go deeper to find out why you see the world this way. You must ask yourself, "What does my mindset or perception stem from?"

Children are as impressionable as they are innocent. We know that during the formative years of life, as children are exploring, learning, and growing, they are also connecting what happens in the world around them to themselves, holding what child psychologists call an egocentric view. They are placing themselves in the middle of situations and scenarios, both good and bad, even though most of the time these situations don't have anything to do with them.

Mom and Dad are fighting; it must be my fault. Mom and Dad are happy today; I must be doing good.

Divorce. Sickness. Disease. Addiction. It is not the event that happens in our lives that determines our perspective but rather how we internalize the event. Blaming ourselves for something happening creates shame, guilt, and doubt. If it is not properly handled and worked through, then shame, guilt, and doubt are carried over and become our working model for all our adult relationships.

When we enter into a relationship with guilt, shame, and doubt, we will perpetuate those things. The tendency to live out what we predict or what is the result of our doings or expectations is called *self-fulfilling prophecy.* Before long, our working model in the context of relationships starts to overflow into how we view ourselves. This working model becomes a false belief or incorrect view of ourselves. It is at this point that our self-proclaimed issues arise. The diagram on the next page illustrates this.

Negative or traumatic event; internalization of event; working model; false belief; not good enough (acting like not good enough); not getting a good job; not getting a partner who values you. *Living out what you perpetuate.*

Yikes! When we operate under a false understanding of ourselves, we act according to that belief. If we believe we are worthless, not good enough, or unlovable, we will act that way. Sometimes, we know we are acting in a way that shows how we feel about ourselves, but more often than not, we are searching for things that match our viewpoint of ourselves. We strive to have our reality match our perception (even if it is a skewed, wrong, and horribly inaccurate perception). So in pursuit of confirming what we believe to be true, we often create the chaos ourselves. That is an example of what happens when we focus too much on the wrong things and let the fallen ways of the world influence us. It would be like a caterpillar eating all the wrong things in preparation to enter the cocoon. Filling ourselves up with the wrong ideas and false teachings will lead to these false perceptions of ourselves.

I have to share something with you. I have a very complicated relationship with food. I've had food issues for years. I either binge eat until I'm so full I feel sick or I restrict myself to eating barely anything for a few days. When it comes to food, I live in the land of two extremes: either I am all in or all out. A cheat day quickly becomes a cheat week for me. Once I figured out my dysfunctional pattern, I did my own digging into my childhood to investigate why I have such an unhealthy relationship with food. What I recall is a specific time when my eating created shame, and that shame created a false belief of my worth. Shame is not from God, but our worth is. Our worth comes from God and God alone.

I remember going to the kitchen to get a second or third serving of ice cream (even as I child I looked to food for comfort), and my dad saw me and proceeded to make cow noises (among other derogatory comments). As I scooped out my ice cream, I felt so ashamed. I felt like I was fat and ugly and that it was all I was going to be. Even now I can place myself back in that moment, and I'm still that same hurt, scared little girl.

Like most little girls, I yearned for my daddy's approval and acceptance. I wanted him to be proud of me, treasure me, and adore me. Did he? Maybe in his own unique way he did. Addiction is a nasty monster; as he was fighting with his own demons, he inevitably withdrew from our family. He became less of a man and more of an empty shell as he was dragged into the pit and decided it wasn't worth trying to climb out. What I never got from my earthy father as a child is what we receive from our heavenly Father—love, acceptance, value, worth.

Now is it my dad's fault that I have struggled with eating and my weight all my life? No, it's not. It is, however, a memory that I can look back on and see that how I internalized my relationship with food as a child is not that much different as an adult. It allows me to pinpoint my own false beliefs around food and navigate my environment safely as an adult. This is one example of how we use awareness in our everyday lives. This awareness of what is going on around us is a good thing to keep in mind when you are either a caterpillar or in a cocoon.

When I say cocoon, I'm referring to a place in your life—maybe a physical place or a situation or circumstance that is hard and maybe even painful. It might be a storm in the sea of life that is thrashing you about, and you just can't quite seem to catch your breath (or even catch a break, for that matter). This cocoon literally could be a time of isolation and separation from others or a feeling that God isn't near. This could also refer to life events over which you have no control and ones that affect your everyday life or cause pain, hurt, worry, or fear. The thing we want to push away or pretend doesn't exist can also be our cocoon. But the key is that we are aware of what we are going through and take steps to process through it. (Don't worry, we will talk more about our cocoon later.)

Once you can see the piece of food stuck in your teeth, you remove it. You can also become aware of what issues you struggle with and seek to maintain your environment. Our internal beliefs manifest themselves into our reality in the form of triggers. *We move to avoid pain, and we move to make sense of the world around us.*

Triggers refer to anything in your environment that spark a memory, thought, or feeling based on your false belief. When we know what potential triggers exist in our everyday lives, we tend to walk around in a mental state of being hyperaware. Being hyperaware means you can pick out what triggers your false beliefs more easily than other people can. Even though you can share the same trigger with someone, your reason for why that is a trigger differs. A trigger can be an external object, a memory, or even words you hear. These triggers can be evidence that we are still in caterpillar thinking if we allow them to set us off.

Trigger as an external object: You see a bottle of vodka on the side of the road, and it is the same kind your alcoholic father used to drink. This elicits anger and bitterness since he ultimately took his addiction to the grave, and you are mad at him for it.

Trigger as memory: Decorating for Christmas brings up other memories of happier holidays when you were all together as a family. You start to feel sad that things are nothing like that these days as your family is torn apart.

Trigger as words you hear: When your husband asks you what you did today, it triggers your insecurity to feel like you have to prove yourself to him. (That stems from the core belief of not feeling good enough.)

These triggers ignite a feeling or response in us and are strongly related to memory flashbacks, but not always. Our minds are very interesting as we learn associations based on repeated exposure. These repeated exposures serve as cues to elicit certain behaviors or responses from us. Our immediate response to our triggers is largely due to our general heightened alertness. Our body is conditioned to either fight or flee when we perceive threats, and since we see these triggers as threats, our bodies respond accordingly. It does not matter whether the threat is real or perceived; our physiological arousal will be the same. Therefore, it is important to be aware of your false beliefs and triggers.

The upside to this heightened alertness is that once you are aware of the trigger, you can do something about it. Depending on the type of trigger, you can remove it, remove yourself from it, or change the association.

Here are some more examples of how a false belief feeds triggers from your environment, and the two just continue to play off each other.

False Belief: not good enough   *possible triggers:* bad grade, criticism
False Belief: worthlessness   *possible triggers:* perfectionism, control issues
False Belief: unlovable   *possible triggers:* harsh words from others, toxic relationship, enabling

What do you notice about most of these triggers? *Many of them are behaviors or identities we take on ourselves.* Perfectionism and attempting to control are choices we make. Staying in an unhealthy relationship or enabling others are choices we make. Keep in mind that it may be easier to identify your habits or patterns of behavior rather than your false belief. Here are some questions you may ask yourself when attempting to understand a false belief you've been carrying around with you:

1. What are some common words, behaviors, or thoughts that spark a negative, emotional response? What is your response to these things?
2. Is there a memory from your childhood when you remember feeling this way?
3. How do you cope with your emotions? How do you handle stress?

Awareness and understanding of your false beliefs and triggers are really just the tip of the iceberg. Knowing what shapes your perspective isn't enough to change it; you have to be willing to take the steps needed for lasting growth and change. It isn't about discipline or having more willpower; it is shifting your perspective and thoughts on change and being open to the Holy Spirit's transformation.

When the caterpillar becomes aware of its surroundings, it isn't afraid to find a branch to spin a cocoon around itself. It's a commitment to obedience and moving forward. It isn't afraid of change but is ready to embrace it. It doesn't run from forming a cocoon, opting instead to stay a caterpillar for its entire life. Remember our metaphor of the caterpillar eating the truth as preparation for the cocoon. At this point, it is full of the truth from the right sources and has become aware of its personal struggle in our fallen world, able to pinpoint triggers and adjust its responses. It is faced with uncertainty for the next step, but it is ready and willing, having faith in God to lead it.

In the following story, can you identify the false belief, the trigger, the emotional response, and the associated behavior?

> *When the woman saw that the fruit of the tree was good for food and pleasing to the eye, and desirable for gaining wisdom, she took some and ate it. She also gave some to her husband, who was with her, and he ate it. Then the eyes of both of them were opened, and they realized they were naked; so they sewed fig leaves together and made coverings for themselves.*
>
> —Gen. 3:6–7

Once Adam and Eve realized they were naked, they covered up. Awareness led to an action because it was fueled by an unpleasant emotion (feeling ashamed). Awareness should always lead us to act. I'm going to be extremely honest here—your false beliefs, your way of handling things, and how you perceive things can all be summed up in one word: pride. When I say pride, I'm not referring only to an inflated sense of self. Pride is also viewing yourself as less than you are. If how you view yourself differs from how God sees you, that is the starting point of false beliefs and skewed perception.

We need to see ourselves as God sees us. When He looks at us, He sees the beautiful butterflies that He has already created us to be. I can say anything, and I can type this, but who God has called you to be and His plan for your life won't make sense or even seem like something you want until you have a firm grasp of what it means to *not* be in Christ and still living for self.

To be fully aware of your shortcomings and false beliefs, you must recognize who you are apart from God.

I love ice cream, and I don't think that will ever change. I also know that ice cream can trigger impulsive binge-eating episodes for me, so for that reason, I don't keep it in the house. I don't want to tempt myself in that way or test my willpower. With willpower alone, I will fail every time. With willpower alone, *you* will fail every time.

There is a reason that Philippians 4:13 (NLT) says, "I can do everything through Christ, who gives me strength." We are powerful and victorious in Christ, but trying to fight our battles alone will leave us discouraged and defeated every time.

I can't stop the cycle of binge eating, feeling worthless about myself, and then eating more to cope. I simply can't fix myself. You can't fix yourself, either. Not even the best self-help book on the market can truly help us. You see, our awareness of sin is a two-sided coin. We're aware of our transgressions, and we're also aware of our inability to fix them on our own. That is when acceptance must happen. Our awareness of whatever God has revealed as our sticking points is only helpful if we are willing to put action behind it. But before we can start to act, we need to accept who we are and who we are not in light of Christ—and who we were before Christ.

CHAPTER 4

Accepting Yourself as a Caterpillar ... Temporarily

I t is hard to look in the mirror, see all my flaws, and still try to accept myself. Being aware of them makes me want to do something to get rid of them, but instead, I work to accept them. I am working to look in the mirror and look beyond the physical marks on my body and instead focus on the reasons for those marks and what joy I have because of what came out of those physical scars—my two beautiful children. Many people, women in particular, look at their bodies in disgust, hating what they see and wishing to look different. I will tell you right now that your physical flaws, false beliefs, and skewed perception of self don't make you a bad person or any worse than others around you.

Do not get caught in the comparison trap. You are not bad for thinking this way about yourself or previously being unaware of the triggers you face. When it comes to negative thoughts we've thought about ourselves for so long and subsequently lived out, we are all on equal playing fields. Don't compare your scars with others. We all carry them differently, but they are there. The Bible tells us that apart from God, we are dead in our sins. Even if we have a relationship with God, sin and temptation are still there because our enemy is lurking, waiting to devour us. We are never immune to this broken world; instead, we respond, knowing our fallen nature and need for a Savior.

> *As for you, you were dead in your transgressions and sins, in which you used to live when you followed the ways of this world and of the ruler of the kingdom of the air, the spirit who is now at work in those who are disobedient. All of us also lived among them at one time, gratifying the cravings of our flesh and following its desires and thoughts. Like the rest, we were by nature deserving of wrath. But because of his great love for us, God, who is rich in mercy, made us alive with Christ even when we were dead in transgressions—it is by grace you have been saved. And God raised us up with Christ and seated us with him in the heavenly realms in Christ Jesus, in order that in the coming ages he might show the incomparable riches of his grace, expressed in his kindness to us in Christ Jesus. For it is by grace you have been saved, through faith—and this is not from yourselves, it is the gift of God—not by works, so that no one can boast. For we are God's handiwork, created in Christ Jesus to do good works, which God prepared in advance for us to do.*
>
> —Eph. 2:1–10

In my life before Christ, I lived for me. I did whatever I wanted, said whatever I felt, and pursued things for my own selfish gain. I didn't know I was in sin because everyone else around me did the same things I did and acted the same way. I honestly didn't know life could be different or that there was even another way. I was merely existing, not living. That all changed one summer in my early 20s.

At that concert where I gave my life to Christ, someone talked about how in sin you often feel like you are just going through the motions of life but constantly feel so empty. That person said that being lost was the best way to describe it; that is, not knowing where you're going or what you're doing. Living with an emptiness and hopelessness, you try to fill the void the best you can with the ways of this world. I describe it as trying to climb up a down escalator—endless, frustrating, and exhausting because you don't go anywhere.

I didn't know my way of life was so wrong or so bad. Sure, I knew that binge drinking and partying probably weren't the greatest uses of my time, but I honestly didn't think I was that bad. I reasoned that I was, for the most part, a good person. I maintained a 3.5 GPA in college, and I was a caring and loving friend. What took me a while to understand, though, is that none of that mattered. We all sin and fall short of the glory of God (Rom. 3:23). Our good deeds apart from God are nothing more than "filthy rags" (Isa. 64:6). *Ouch!* Once my sinful lifestyle and need for God to save me from myself was pointed out to me, I couldn't just ignore it.

> *For all have sinned and fall short of the glory of God.*
>
> —Rom. 3:23

> *All of us have become like one who is unclean,*
> *and all our righteous acts are like filthy rags;*
> *we all shrivel up like a leaf,*
> *and like the wind our sins sweep us away.*
>
> —Isa. 64:6

When I felt convicted about how I was living my life, I really felt it. It was crushing and heart-wrenching to admit that I was living apart from God and that I needed Him. I was very stubborn and independent, so I didn't think I needed anyone. But when I humbled myself at the foot of the cross, repented of my sins, and asked God to change me, He met me right where I was, and that was my hatching point.

Accepting that you are where you are and not trying to pretend to be better or do better on your own is what God is begging us to do. He knows our sins, false beliefs, and struggles, but He wants us to openly confess them and ask Him to bridge the gap between our weakness and His strength. He wants us to call on Him while we are caterpillars and especially when we are in cocoons. When we are weak, when we feel like we can't go on, that is when we need to call out to God the most.

> *But he said to me, "My grace is sufficient for you, for my power is made perfect in weakness." Therefore, I will boast all the more gladly about my weaknesses, so that Christ's power may rest on me.*
>
> —2 Cor. 12:9

Not only are we called to be okay with our weaknesses but to boast in them because it is in those weaknesses that God shines His strength through us. We have to know our weaknesses and willingly surrender them to God instead of trying to fix them ourselves. In this way, we glorify God in a way that keeps us humble and keeps Him as Lord.

Surrender. It's a word that many people don't like. The idea of surrendering or even submitting to God is enough to make us run the other direction. It's one thing to admit that you are walking in sin and need help from someone greater than yourself, but it is another thing to surrender yourself to the working of the Holy Spirit. You must admit that you can't change yourself. You must be willing to give up control of your life and rest entirely in the arms of our trustworthy God. He won't let you see how it all plays out; instead, He calls you to have faith in Him and His purpose for you.

This is not unlike being spiritually blind or unaware because after you have been in darkness and sin for so long, when your eyes are finally opened, you can see clearly for the first time. It truly is the epitome of

---

You must be willing to give up control of your life and rest entirely in the arms of our trustworthy God.

---

bringing you out of darkness into the light to see yourself as God sees you, apart from Him a sinner and with Him still a sinner but a worthy and valuable recipient of His grace.

Food for Thought Questions:
- What are the struggles, worries, fears, and insecurities that prevent you from seeing clearly who God has made you to be? We will talk more about false beliefs in the next chapter. We will discuss how the words we say or accept that others say affect our view of ourselves and willingness to surrender control.
- How can you be open and honest with God about your sin?
- What do you need to surrender to Him today?

The truth is that the Holy Spirit desires to lead you in *every* area of life. He can't do that if you don't readily offer that up to Him. Your finances. Your career. Your marriage. Your health. Have you surrendered these areas and asked God to move on your behalf? What areas are you still holding onto, trying to control?

If you have yet to surrender yourself completely to Christ, I invite you to recite this short prayer, giving God permission to move in all areas of your life:

> Heavenly Father, I thank You for loving me. I thank You for accepting me just the way I am and sending Your Son Jesus to save me. I release all my worries, fears, insecurities, and doubts to You. From this point on, I will stop trying to control my life and let You control my life. Teach me to trust You. Teach me to surrender myself fully to You. I declare that I will see You move in my marriage, my health, my finances, and my relationships. Thank You for the work You are already doing in my life and the work You are going to do. Lead me to a deeper relationship with You and a greater understanding. In Jesus's name. Amen.

CHAPTER 5

The Label Maker

I love labels. I'm referring to the labels that you make to identify objects, not the labels we give ourselves. I like to be able to look in my kitchen or in my closet and know what is in a box before I open it. But there are certain types of labels I don't like—the ones we give ourselves or allow others to give us. I was bullied in the second grade, and my mother told me to tell the girl who constantly made fun of me and called me names that "sticks and stones may break my bones, but words will never hurt me. I'm rubber and you're glue; whatever you say bounces off me and sticks to you."

While this is a catchy rhyme, it is wrong. Words *do* hurt. They often have a lasting impact on our minds as well as our hearts. They aren't something we can just shrug off or forget, especially when negative words are spoken over us. When my dad made those derogatory comments about me, they stuck with me. When the bully called me fat, lazy, and stupid, those words also stuck. The more others said these things to me, the more I believed them. Not only do the words that others speak over us hurt, but the words we say to ourselves pierce just as deep, if not deeper.

I don't know about you, but I've said some nasty things about myself. The names I've called myself I wouldn't call even my worst enemy. So why do we treat ourselves so poorly? How have the labels we've placed on ourselves and the ones we've let stick determine our ability to accept ourselves?

You Are Special by Max Lucado is the story of how labels affect us and how to stop them from dictating our lives once and for all. It is geared toward children, but I think it is just as important for adults to read and really let the message of what our worth and value are to our Creator sink in. Here is a summary of the story:

> As we step into the Wemmick village, we meet a small, wooden creature named Punichello. Punichello, like the other Wemmick people, lives his life in pursuit of being awarded stars to wear. Stars are given to those who have a special talent or are pretty. The Wemmicks are responsible for awarding these stars to each other. If you are not awarded stars, you are given dots. Dots mean you don't deserve a star and aren't as good as the others. Punichello racks up so many dots trying to be someone he's not that he reaches the point where he no longer wants to go outside.
>
> When he has to go outside, people see all his dots and give him more. They decide that since he has so many dots, he deserves more. Punichello starts to believe that he isn't a good Wemmick because other people tell him that. Then one day he meets another Wemmick named Lucia who doesn't have any stars or dots. Lucia tells Punichello to take a visit to the woodcarver, Eli, to learn how to make the dots and stars not stick.
>
> When Punichello meets Eli, he learns more about why Eli made him the way he did. Eli assures him by saying that what the Wemmicks think doesn't matter. All that matters is what he thinks, and he thinks Punichello is pretty special.

Whoa! Time out. Punichello spends his life trying to earn the approval of others, and Eli, his maker, tells him all that matters is what he thinks. Eli thinks Punichello is pretty special because he made him. In the story, Eli is God, who makes us unique and special for a purpose. Punichello asks him how he is special because he can't do anything and doesn't have talents like the others. Eli responds by telling him, "Because you're mine, that's why you matter to me."

> *Yet you, LORD, are our Father.*
> *We are the clay, you are the potter;*
> *we are all the work of your hand.*
>
> —Isa. 64:8

All that matters is that we matter to God. We are created to love God and to love others. Punichello has a lot to learn when it comes to not letting what others think affect him. Eli tells him something that I think we could also benefit from.

The stickers only stick if you let them.

The labels only stick if you let them. The names you've been called and the words that have been spoken over you only have power if you give them power. How can you stop letting those words control you today? How different would your life be, how different would *you* be if you could let those words just bounce off you instead of stick to you? Caterpillar thinking focuses on those words and gives power. We limit ourselves when we listen and perform based on other people's expectations.

What does it mean to stop living under the labels and start living under your Maker?

At the very end of the story, Eli tells Punichello to only care what he thinks and not what others think, and that it will take some time for all those dots to fall off as he learns how to respond to others' opinions of him.

I have a friend who is a great example of what can happen when we allow God to remove a label that someone else placed on us as a child. When she was a child in art class, her art teacher told her she had zero artistic talent and ability. So as a result of believing those words spoken over her as a child, she always believed she wasn't artistic and steered clear of doing anything that had to do with art well into adulthood. Recently, all those lies she believed about what she could or could not do came crashing down after she started seeing an art therapist who encouraged her to start painting to help her process things from her past. As she started to paint, she started to enjoy it and now regularly shares her paintings on Instagram and is even looking into selling her paintings on Etsy. God took away that label and limitation that was placed on her and is now redeeming her past by giving her the courage and space to share her story through art.

Living with Labels Creates Limitations

If we only see ourselves as what other people say instead of how God sees us, we close off a large portion of ourselves and the potential God has for us. In order to tap into this, we must be real—*really real*—and ready.

What would it look like if you approached God right now where you are in your journey and were honest with Him? Don't try to cover up or straighten up before you approach Him; instead, give Him permission to work in your life on your behalf just as you are right now. God meets us right where we are and pours out His grace in our lives. No matter how beat up, worn down, or full of labels we are, He takes special care and consideration, slowly peeling off those labels and making us into who He has created us to be.

Sometimes, it's hard to escape the labels we live under and stop believing we are no good to God as we are now and need to be better before He can really use us. Where did we get the idea that we don't matter to God as we are right now? This largely has to do with how society tells us what we need to be or achieve in order to be happy or worthy. These if-only statements really get us in trouble when we're talking about being acceptable and pleasing in God's eyes right now.

If only I was 10 years younger . . .

If only I was prettier . . .

If only I was 20 pounds lighter . . .

Guess the second part of those statements.

. . . then I would finally be happy.

Companies that market weight loss supplements, or any company that makes money off your insecurities, loves to tell you that you just need their product, and you'll finally be happy. Well, I hate to burst your bubble, but no, you won't. When we look at happiness this way, we place our happiness in what we believe our value to be (e.g., I would be more valuable if I was younger, prettier, and thinner).

I set out to lose weight before my wedding. I went on a very restrictive diet and started exercising twice a day. I killed myself in the gym and cursed myself if my daily morning weigh-in was more than I wanted. When I met the initial weight loss goal I set for myself, I didn't feel happy or satisfied. Instead, I set a new number and a new goal, and I beat myself up when I didn't achieve it.

Your value isn't in who you will become;
it is in who you are right now.

Whether you are a caterpillar, cocoon, or butterfly, you matter to God right now. God made you the way you are for a reason, and He isn't going to love you any differently if you are thinner, younger, or prettier. He doesn't love you or value you more on the days you choose salads over cupcakes or even when you manage to not lose your temper with your children. His love isn't based on performance, but rather it is based on grace and grace alone. We will mess up. We will make mistakes. We "all have sinned and fall short of the glory of God" (Rom. 3:23). We all are in desperate need of a Savior to save us from our sins and inequities.

That is where the power of salvation through faith in Jesus Christ comes into play. Yes, there is the potential we have in Christ and how He will use us to advance His kingdom, but He desires for us to know what He thinks about us and why He created us. Getting back to the main story reminds us that we have been chosen and set apart, and it is never too late to commit or recommit our lives to Christ. It's like getting keys to a brand new car but not knowing how to drive. He doesn't want us to take our keys and run the other direction. He is there to show us and be with us every step of the way. He tells us when to put our foot on the gas or when it is time to pump the brakes. He shows us which way to turn and when we need to stay in our lane.

I encourage you to read Ephesians 2 repeatedly and let it sink in that God loved you even when you were dead in your sins, and He came to bridge the gap on your behalf. He is asking you to surrender control to Him. The question to ask yourself at this step is this: Is God's grace enough to cover my (insert false belief or label you've believed)? It's time to get into the cocoon to be transformed by God.

If you believe you are ready to present God your true self, mess and all and have Him accept you for you and shower you with mercy and grace, then I encourage you to take the first step today. If you are ready to stop worrying about the labels that others give you and start focusing on the only label that matters—a child of God—then you are ready to enter the cocoon.

INSIDE THE
Cocoon

We're now in the third stage of the life cycle. The formal name is the pupa, or chrysalis. This is when the caterpillar is in the cocoon for a determined amount of time, enough time for the full transformation to occur. The caterpillar actually spins and creates the cocoon to go into by itself. On the outside, it looks like nothing is going on, but on the inside, the caterpillar is undergoing many rapid and radical changes. It will be reduced to a pile of goo and completely broken down on a cellular level before it will emerge as a butterfly.

When we are in our own cocoons, we may have a period of darkness and loneliness. Changing into who God called us to be is hard and grueling work. In our own lives, it can seem as though we are being broken down so God can build us back up. While inside the cocoon, we have to come to the conclusion that we are not enough and that God is the only one who can sustain us. The spiritual growth we desire to have has to come from a place of self-reflection and humility along with the correct posture of heart. We have to be able and willing to take a hard look at ourselves in order to be able to grow and change. Often this change is painful, but it is well worth it when we break out of the cocoon, or rather when God takes us out of the cocoon. There are a few key things we can keep in mind when we feel trapped in our cocoon, as we will discuss in the following chapter.

CHAPTER 6

Being Authentic about Your Struggle

Inner work is hard work. Tearing down strongholds, rejecting false beliefs, and everything that goes on inside our cocoon can be painful, but when we emerge in Christ as beautiful butterflies, we find we are free to be ourselves and live out our God-given purposes. Many times, this involves taking our mess, our hard situations, and our struggles and using them for His glory. That starts with vulnerability and transparency.

When we struggle, we need to be authentic about that struggle, trust the process, and be honest about the process.

How are you today?
I'm fine. How are you?
I'm fine, thanks.

This could be a conversation between any two women anywhere. It could be between people who don't know each other very well just as much as it could be between good friends. How many times have you have a conversation like that with either a neighbor or even your best friend? In my own experience (my husband can vouch for this), when I say fine, I'm not really fine; instead, I'm trying to hide or cover up something deeper that is going on.

There is something to be said about the words *I'm fine*. Arguably, whoever says they're fine usually is not. Pastor Dave Willis from the church we attended in Georgia once gave an entire sermon series on the word *fine*. He purported that fine stands for:

F – FAKE
I – IGNORING
N – NEGLECTING
E – EVADING

So if you say you're fine, you are doing one of those things. This is a hard truth to realize. We walk around wearing the I'm-fine face instead of speaking the truth to each other. The real you is always better than the fake you. As we start to look more at what it means to be authentic and transparent, I hope you can see that the benefits of being authentic far outweigh the costs.

Authenticity and transparency are attributes I strongly value in others. I jokingly say that authenticity is my jam. Call it the introvert in me, but I prefer deep conversation to surface-level talk any day of the week. I guess that's why making new friends can somewhat be a challenge. To be authentic and real with others is to accept who you are and be okay showing others the real you. We naturally care what others think and want to make a good impression. There is something to be said about putting yourself out there and not being accepted by your peers. The good news is that even though this is scary at first, it can start to feel less intimidating the more you do it.

Why do you think it's easier to pretend everything is okay instead of being transparent with one another? Why is it easier to say that our cocoon time isn't a struggle or hard and brush it off as no big deal? (Hint: Remember those false beliefs we talked about before?) Below are two main fears that may fuel our inability to be transparent with people around us.

Fear of rejection. We all want to be liked. When we put ourselves out there, we become vulnerable. Our realness can be rejected or misunderstood. I'm sure you can remember a time when you were a little too real, and what resulted from that interaction was rejection.

Fear of judgment. As a mom, I feel this all the time, even though I'm 100 percent sure that every mom in the world feels like she is being judged some of the time. The truth is that we are all so worried about being judged by other moms that we don't have time to throw stones. Or maybe you aren't being paranoid and are really being judged by other moms. So what? Remember what we said about other people's opinions? *Don't let them stick.*

When we become more open and transparent, our walls come down as we start to let others in. However, we also start to be on guard more and become more hyper-focused on threats to our vulnerability (triggers, anyone?). The fear of rejection and the fear of judgment are two barriers to authenticity that have the potential to freeze us. These barriers can keep us in bondage if we're not careful. Just like being aware and accepting of who we are, authenticity must be done intentionally and with safe people; otherwise, it will not bear the right kind of fruit and can easily become manipulated and misunderstood.

We need to be cautious inside our cocoon. While we are transforming into beautiful new creatures, we are indeed still fragile and in vulnerable states. While going through those hard and painful times, sometimes we tend to say too much too soon, and in our effort to cultivate community, we project ourselves as nosy or even needy.

Shortly after moving to Colorado, I met a young woman, and we just seemed to instantly hit it off as friends. Our babies were only a few months apart, so when she invited me to go with her to baby time at the library, I happily obliged.

Another woman she had been friendly with started chatting with us before baby time, and everything was going well until she mentioned she was pregnant (she had a six-month-old baby and was expecting again.) Now I know you may be thinking I probably made some off-the-wall comment or something like that, but it was actually quite the opposite. Suddenly, I wanted to know everything about her pregnancy—if she was breastfeeding when she got pregnant or if she got her period back before she got pregnant. I wanted to know because I wanted to get pregnant again, so I was hoping she would share her secrets with me. She was nice and answered my questions but also strategically moved herself across the room, purposefully avoiding me and my rapid-fire questions.

I was so transparent and authentic; I just laid it all out there. So what was the problem? What happened? I thought authenticity was supposed to be appreciated and even reciprocated. I had made a crucial mistake. I forgot that not everyone is as comfortable with authenticity as I am. In this instance, it wasn't so much about my level of realness as it was about the fact that I didn't respect the toe-dipping period of getting to know someone. Just because she had determined that my friend was safe did not automatically mean I was safe. I explain more about the toe-dipper theory below.

In our struggles and messes, we do need to be authentic and transparent with one another; there is no doubt about that. However, there is a time and place for that, as I suggest below.

How do you enter a swimming pool? Do you dip your toe in to check the temperature of the water before you jump in? Do you jump in without checking the temperature? Or do you step into the water little by little, going deeper as you get more comfortable?

Toe-dippers. You want to know quite literally what you are getting yourself into before you make the mistake of jumping into a freezing-cold pool. The problem with only dipping our toe in is that toes barely go below the surface. Water is always warmer on the surface and cooler underneath. If we only take time to test it with a toe, we only get part of the picture.

Jumpers. You don't care what the temperature of the water is. You see a swimming pool and want in. You're not paying much attention to the possibility of the water being colder than you'd like since you are focused more on the fun and experience of the water than your comfort. Your motto is to jump in and deal with the consequences later.

Step-by-steppers. You are cautious and want no surprises, so you feel better just going into the pool little by little. That means you may be waist-deep in water but still haven't gotten your hair wet or put your face in, thus missing out on the full experience.

Which one most closely relates to you in new social situations? When you meet new people, how are you likely to react and respond? Are you a toe-dipper or a jumper? Are you a step-by-stepper? All these questions are important in determining how safe a person is and how likely you are to take off your I'm-fine face so someone can get to know the real you.

Just like being at the swimming pool, we need to not get ahead of ourselves (like I did at baby time) and take the time to survey the scene (in this case, people) to make sure they are safe. The misstep I took was because my need for authenticity stemmed from a need for validation and approval instead of genuine openness. My need to reach out and make a real friend was what sparked the friendship between me and my close friend. A friend of a friend also seems a little safer than a stranger, but we should still proceed with caution.

Survey the Scene

When looking for a potential friend, research suggests that we gravitate toward someone who is similar to us. Evolutionists claim that if we see someone we perceive as like us, there is a level of immediate comfort and security. We believe that since they are like us, we can trust them. Initially, this can be a very good thing until you start comparing your lives more closely and realize that they are, in fact, very different from you. While similarities can spark a friendship, it is truly the differences that make it special. Perhaps you've heard this quote from Pastor Steven Furtick of Elevation Church, and it is so true: "The reason we struggle with insecurity is because we compare our behind-the-scenes with everyone else's highlight reel."[3]

Don't compare your behind-the-scenes with everyone else's highlight reel.

This is especially true in our age when Facebook and Instagram are platforms to post about your "perfect" life. We can't help but be depressed when we compare our lives to others around us. While we identify safe people to share our lives with and be authentic with in person, technology can serve as a safeguard to judgment or rejection. That means that opening up with others online feels easier. No matter whether you are being authentic online or in person, it is important to know when to share and when not to share.

Safe People and Sharing Appropriately

I so wish that everyone you decided to be authentic and transparent with would respond with equal levels of authenticity and acceptance, but that doesn't always happen. Sharing your story with safe people in a safe space doesn't always mean your authenticity will be reciprocated. If you share too much too soon, people will perceive it as neediness, and if you don't share enough, people might think you are rigid, unemotional, or closed off. Remember, at the core we all want to be liked and accepted by others, so if you are still living to please others and looking to them instead of God for approval, your oversharing may not yield the result you intended. Again, this can suggest you may still have a caterpillar-like mindset.

---

3. Steven Furtick, *Goodreads*, https://www.goodreads.com/quotes/1128481-the-reason-we-struggle-with-insecurity-is-because-we-compare.

Ways to cultivate authenticity:

- Look for commonalities and expand on them (e.g., moms of toddlers discuss what it is like and how they tackle certain toddler topics with each other).
- Try to avoid closed-ended questions that can be answered with a simple yes or no. If you really want to expand your friendship, you have to open up and ask questions that require an answer beyond yes or no.
- Follow the piece-by-piece rule. Share things about yourself little by little instead of all at once. For instance, when I meet someone for the first time, I rarely open with "I am an adult child of an alcoholic." Instead, I let the conversation flow naturally, and when the topic of family comes up, I approach it carefully, giving personal detail but also not overwhelming the listener with too many details.

Let's now turn our attention to why our authentic story is crucial for our spiritual growth—why it matters in the cocoon and outside the cocoon.

Contentment in the Cocoon

> *I am not saying this because I am in need, for I have learned to be content whatever the circumstances. I know what it is to be in need, and I know what it is to have plenty. I have learned the secret of being content in any and every situation, whether well fed or hungry, whether living in plenty or in want.*
>
> —Phil. 4:11–12

Look at the above verses. How many of us can say the same thing, that we have truly learned to be content in plenty and in want? How can someone be just as content in either circumstance? The idea that we can learn to be content as we are in the cocoon or enduring a season of difficulty may seem impossible for some. Contentment is less about being happy and more about being holy.

Think of where you are right now in your life. Are you content in your circumstances? What is contributing to that feeling of contentment?

The truth is that as Christians, we are called to be holy (set apart), and one of the ways we do that is by learning to be content in our circumstances. That is hard to do when the world wants to constantly remind us who we are not and what we do not have. There seems to be something bigger and better, and all roads lead to the fact that some people are smarter, prettier, and more successful than we are.

The Enemy of Contentment Is Comparison

More than comparing physical looks or social status, we often compare our specific circumstances with one another, especially if we feel like we have done everything the same. We don't have any control over our cocoon time, how long a particular period or season of pain and worry might last, but we do have control over how we respond to the process.

Don't fight the cocoon time in your life. Instead, allow God to use that time to restore you and redeem you.

I don't know anyone who would be particularly thankful for tough, unforeseen circumstances such as cancer, divorce, death, debt, and so on, but I do know that it is possible to be thankful in those circumstances.

> *Give thanks in all circumstances; for this is God's will for you in Christ Jesus.*
>
> —1 Thess. 5:18

Give thanks in all circumstances. I love how it says *in* all circumstances and not *for*. It takes the pressure off feeling like I have to thank

God for my intense struggles and helps me think more about how He shows Himself through the things I can be thankful for. I'm not saying you need to be thankful when tragedy strikes but that even in the midst of your worst-case scenario, you can still find something to be thankful for. Notice that it also says "this is God's will for you in Christ Jesus." That means that apart from God, it is impossible to be thankful in extreme circumstances.

We are content inside the cocoon because God is with us. We may not like it, not understand it, and wish that this dark time would go away, but through it all, God is with us. Even in the hard times (yes, even in the binding cocoon), He will give us His peace that transcends all understanding.

> *Do not be anxious about anything, but in every situation, by prayer and petition, with thanksgiving, present your requests to God. And the peace of God, which transcends all understanding, will guard your hearts and your minds in Christ Jesus.*
>
> —Phil. 4:6–7

CHAPTER 7

Your Authentic Story: Butterfly Emerging

We all have a story. We all have a testimony. There are key components of sharing our stories that are crucial for spiritual growth. Before we dive into what we need to do when we share our story, we need to first ask ourselves this: Why do I want to share my story? Asking this question right away sets the stage for us to determine the best approach to sharing our story with others.

The need for you to share your story is greater than the need to stay guarded.

Let that sink in for a second. You have gone through or are experiencing a unique set of circumstances that can potentially help a person get through what you have already gone through or at the very least assure them they are not alone. Butterflies don't fly without purpose. Sharing your stories with the right people can open up opportunities for growth and healing.

Opening up to each other is scary. The struggle is real when it comes to trying to be your authentic self without looking like a hot mess. Society teaches us we need to be strong and put together and not share our struggles or worries with others. This philosophy is wrong. Strength isn't about putting on a happy face and pretending everything is okay. True strength is asking for help when needed and not being afraid to share your weaknesses with others. This is what separates a butterfly impostor from a real-deal, transformed butterfly.

If there was no benefit to authenticity and sharing our story, then it wouldn't be so hard. The enemy (Satan) would love nothing more than to keep us in darkness to our struggles and our story. He often does this by creating shame and doubt in us (sound familiar?). As a result of this shame and doubt, we start to isolate ourselves. We start to think we are weird or different and that no one could possibly understand our pain, so we shut ourselves off to the outside world, deciding it is easier to be alone than misunderstood.

If Satan can isolate us, he can influence us.

The lies of the enemy hit us hard in that dark place, so we need to expose the things the enemy wants us to keep hidden to the light of Christ. When we bring those situations and circumstances out of the darkness and expose them, first to God and then to others, we start to grow spiritually. When we expose our shortcoming to the healing power of Christ, our story isn't just our story anymore; it's our personal account of God's goodness. This is the power of living from the butterfly perspective. Shining our light can be as simple as a kind gesture to a stranger or telling our testimony, whatever it may be, in front of a crowd, knowing that it must be done from an authentic and loving heart.

The light shines in the darkness, and the darkness has not overcome it.

—John 1:5

I can think of many instances in my own life when God demonstrated (and continues to demonstrate) His goodness and faithfulness. The telling of these stories highlights His glory, giving others hope. I once gave a message to a group of Christian military wives on this very topic. I told the story of how I wrote my dad, addressing his addiction, and then how I opened up at our small group only to find out I wasn't alone. Another woman there had also written her dad a letter addressing his addiction. Words cannot even express how I felt once I found out I wasn't alone. I wasn't alone in my struggle as a daughter of an alcoholic. I wasn't alone in my situation. Someone who had gone through exactly what I was facing was there with me. The confidence I had after knowing I wasn't the only one who had to deal with this really helped my faith and helped me grow closer to God in that season. In this woman's story, her dad has been sober for many years and a changed man through the power of Jesus; in my story, God is still trying to get hold of my dad's heart. Regardless of the outcome of our stories, it is nice to be able to walk alongside someone who understands and can help carry the burden.

Carry each other's burdens, and in this way you will fulfill the law of Christ.

—Gal. 6:2

This verse reminds us that we are made for community and to help each other. Each of us has a burden to bear, and while some of us can overshare, others can lean the other way, not wanting to be a burden to others. While some of the hardships we face are things we can carry ourselves, there are other things that weigh us down and become too heavy for us to walk through alone. It's true that some people aren't going to understand your sharing and may misinterpret it as being needy or trying to gain pity and sympathy. For the ones who don't understand you or think you are complaining, that's okay because your story is not for them. Once you can be transparent and share authentically and vulnerably with others without fear of rejection or judgment, you are well on your way to being transformed into the image of Christ.

God Uses the Cocoon to Change Us

And we all, who with unveiled faces contemplate the Lord's glory, are being transformed into his image with ever-increasing glory, which comes from the Lord, who is the Spirit.

—2 Cor. 3:18

Finding a safe space with people who also share with you the hard times they are facing so you can ask for prayer and receive encouragement and advice is a good place to start. Once I saw that it was okay to share with this woman and other members of my small group, it was like I could exhale and just be me. I was safe to share without being judged. Safe people offer support. Safe people offer encouragement through their stories. Through our story, God redeems, God restores, and God reconciles. Sometimes, it's not how we imagined or what we would choose for ourselves, but God's way is always the best way. It's one thing to tell your story on the other side of it, but it's challenging to be completely vulnerable in the here and now, especially if your story is your current season of life. It takes a special leap of faith to be willing to share your story in the middle of it, unable to see how it ends. Remember, the cocoon is temporary, and even though it may seem like it will go on forever, it won't. The end will come, and you will emerge as a new creation in Christ. He wants you to use your story to help others and bring Him glory.

Your struggle is your story. Your story is your past, your present, and your future. While we know what we've lived through and what we're going through, we don't know what lies ahead of us. Never forget that God is the author of your story, and He isn't finished writing it.

I would be remiss if I did not include a caution about sharing someone else's story. There is a time and a place for this type of sharing, and it can be tricky to determine what to share and what not to share. There is something to be said when you hear what someone is going through and you can relate by saying your aunt, mom, sister, or cousin is dealing with the *same thing*; however, in many cases, this isn't your story to share for several reasons.

Confidentiality

The first reason has to do with confidentiality. This is something largely discussed in small groups and Bible studies—what is shared within the group, stays within the group. However, what if you wish to share someone else's story? When you are sharing something about another person, you need permission to do so. Respecting that person's privacy and confidentiality ensures that group will continue to trust you as each member shares more personal things moving forward.

Testimony vs. Story

This is an interesting comparison as many of us don't see a difference between a testimony and a story, especially if both give glory to God. But a first-person account of God's goodness and faithfulness is what makes a testimony. These are the stories of ex-criminals, ex-drug addicts, and cancer survivors that all can testify on God's behalf. These are also the stories of angry moms, prideful excuse makers, and insecure liars whom God redeemed. A second-person story, on the other hand, is the telling of someone else's experience with God. Remember, no one can tell your story like you can because you are the one who lived it.

It can be tempting to share someone else's story, what that person is going through, instead of your own because it is less scary and less vulnerable. It won't do you any favors to close yourself off because while many of our stories share similarities, they are still independent experiences. The butterfly transforms from a caterpillar, but the process looks different for everyone. In the same environment, it might take more or less time for the butterfly to emerge out of the cocoon depending on water and light. This water and light can represent Christ and our response to the Holy Spirit inside us.

While my husband was in a dental residency program, I could share my experience with other resident wives whose husbands were in the same program, but the truth is that our experiences were different. Yes, we shared a common life stage and perhaps some similar woes because our husbands were gone most of the time, but how we chose to respond to the situation was different. We were different people, and our husbands were different people. Our perspectives were different based on our expectations and experiences. Not only do we all have unique stories independent of each other, but we also have specific details of our stories that God uses to speak to others. Whether it is admitting how tired or overwhelmed we feel as moms, the detail of writing a letter to someone, or some other intricate element, it makes us who we are and has value in our lives. That value strikes a chord in another person's life. It's like hearing a sermon and being tuned out for most of it except for a statement that the pastor makes that really stands out and sticks in your mind. Perhaps you don't recall the entire message, but you are captured by the statement that speaks to you. It's not just a take-home message but rather a transforming message. We are transformed so we can help transform others. Make no mistake, though; it is God who does the heavy lifting through us, and we are privileged to be used by Him in our obedience.

> *Therefore go and make disciples of all nations, baptizing them in the name of the Father and of the Son and of the Holy Spirit, and teaching them to obey everything I have commanded you. And surely I am with you always, to the very end of the age.*
>
> —Matt. 28:19–20

Your story is your unique calling card to what God has placed on your life. The scars you bear, both emotionally and physically, tell a story. Never be ashamed of your past since God uses your past to fulfill your purpose. There is purpose in your pain and a message amid your mess. Your story could very well be the key that unlocks healing in another person. Whether it be faith, hope, love, trust, truth, or peace, biblically we are called to be authentic with one another.

> *Therefore each of you must put off falsehood and speak truthfully to your neighbor, for we are all members of one body.*
>
> —Eph. 4:25

Some people, when asked how they are doing, reply with this: Too blessed to be stressed. Do you think there is truth to that statement, or could it be an example of a falsehood?

Are we ever too blessed to be stressed? First, *bless* is a verb. God and others bless us, and we bless others. I know some of you may disagree with me and say that you can feel blessed. Let me ask you a question, though. When you feel blessed, what other emotions come to mind?

Happy. Joyful. Thankful. Loved. While we are blessed 100 percent of the time, are we happy, joyful, and thankful 100 percent of the time? No. That would be impossible. Life has too many ups and downs and unexpected twists and turns for us to be happy all the time. Even though we are blessed by so many things, too blessed to be stressed can be said in an attempt to convince ourselves that we are okay instead of being transparent with the one who asked us. Sometimes, we want

---

Your story could very well be the key that unlocks healing in another person.

---

to stay hidden in our cocoon, the dark place with no one around, not because it is better for us but because we feel safe and think it is easier. Sometimes, in our cocoon we get a false sense of security that we must work hard to overcome and be able to tell it like it is. In my experience, the more you try to convince yourself and others that you are fine, the more you really are not.

Of course, there is a fine line between letting every little thing affect you and pretending that nothing bothers you. As Christians, the Bible tells us that it won't be all smooth sailing for us; instead, we will have trouble as believers.

> *In this world you will have trouble.*
>
> —John 16:33

We see an example of this trouble in the book of Job. I encourage you to read it if you never have. As you go through it, notice how Job responds to what God has for him and also what he does when he receives the less than helpful advice from his wife and friends. It seems as though we always try to pinpoint a reason for suffering because we want out of it, but God is very clear that there are things of this world that we know nothing about; they are a mystery to us and will stay hidden from our knowledge and understanding.

> *The secret things belong to the LORD our God, but the things revealed belong to us and to our children forever, that we may follow all the words of this law.*
>
> —Deut. 29:29

We know suffering and trouble. We live in a broken and fallen world, and the natural consequences of sin include pain, trouble, suffering, and difficulty. We don't have to worry about these things because Jesus conquered death, and grace reminds us that He has overcome the world. That is why we can live out our faith as a butterfly even though we are still stuck in the cocoon. You see, friends, having a butterfly perspective is all about having faith, trust, and confidence in who you are in Christ.

I have told you these things, so that in me you may have
peace. In this world you will have trouble. But take heart! I
have overcome the world.

—John 16:33

So what does this have to do with being too blessed to be stressed? It means that while we are here on earth, we will never be immune to the consequences of sin in our broken world. We will hurt, we will feel pain, and we might be stressed on occasion. When we start to feel overwhelmed and feel we can't handle anymore of what life wants to throw at us, that's when we need to share our story and our authentic self with others. Here is another example from my own life where God used my authenticity to bring healing to my heart.

When I was in dark depression as a newly married person just having moved several states away from my close family and friends, it was hard to be real with the friends I had made just a few months after my move. We have talked about safe people and safe spaces to share, but it can be extremely terrifying to take that first step into being vulnerable. Once I was able to open up about my struggles, I was met with an overwhelming amount of love and support from my new friends. How could these people love and care for me without knowing me for a long time? They showed me love but, more specifically, *Christ's love*. It wasn't sympathy; it was empathy. It wasn't because they felt bad or didn't know what else to do; their love and kindness were from the overflow of their hearts. Helping me through my depression by carrying my burden wasn't a chore for them. It was something they delighted in doing. What I learned from these women during that season is that it is possible to care for and help others with an unwavering compassion, but it is only possible if you are in Christ.

A simple question to ask yourself when attempting to take off your I'm-fine face and deciding whether it is appropriate to be authentic is this: What am I trying to cover up, and what do I not want others to find out about me? Keep in mind that your affinity for pretending things are okay when they are not can very well be related to your false beliefs and even the negative self-talk that you engage in with yourself or others. Being real and authentic takes intentionality and practice. It also looks different for everyone. Having that butterfly perspective is about having a renewed mind and faith. It is about living intentionally and with purpose, confident in who God has created you to be. It is admitting your sin and mistakes and taking steps to grow in those areas of your life.

If you've been authentic and transparent with someone, sharing your story and successes, then you've most likely also talked about your struggles. Accountability with grace is the next step toward spiritual growth and complete metamorphosis.

THE
Butterfly

Once we are who God has transformed us to be, there is no going back. A butterfly cannot physically return to being a caterpillar, acting as it did before the transformation, and neither should we. In God's timing, the struggles we face strengthen us and prepare us for what we need to be authentic and share our story. A butterfly doesn't fly randomly; it flies to a flower to eat and lay eggs. It knows its purpose, and the goal at this stage is to lay as many eggs as possible before it dies. The butterfly has a short life span, typically two weeks or less. It doesn't waste any time fulfilling its purpose before it dies, and neither should we.

CHAPTER 8

The Butterfly Has Emerged, So Now What?

D oing life together—that was the tagline for the small group we attended in Georgia. We did, indeed, do life together. We all rejoiced when babies, books, and marriages happened in our group and cried and prayed when miscarriages, misfortunes, and mistakes happened. While we shared similar life experiences with those people, we also shared a passion and heart for God. It was one thing to admit our struggles with each other and another to admit that we didn't want to live with an issue and wanted to do better. One of those women became my fitness accountability partner. We started swimming laps together and shared our eating habits with each other as a daily check-in.

The act of sharing your struggles with someone else is powerful. In a prayer group I attended, a lady there confessed her struggle with food, and once she talked about her food issues, I knew we would be able to connect on a deeper level. When you share struggles with others, there is a special kind of empathy for each other because we've been in each other's shoes before or are walking in them now. When we are honest about our cocoon experiences, it opens up a way to connect with others that can lead to transformation.

Therefore confess your sins to each other and pray for each other so that you may be healed. The prayer of a righteous person is powerful and effective.

—James 5:16

The confession of our transgressions tears down the I'm-perfect-and-never-mess-up façade and instead gives up hope and support in the form of community and fellowship. Before the friend in my prayer group openly confessed her struggle to me, I saw her as perfect. I saw her as someone who was very in touch with God. I imagined she was silently criticizing me and the words I spoke as I prayed out loud. The enemy wanted me to be intimidated and stay intimidated so I would remain silent and stunned. When she broke down the barrier by offering a genuine confession, everything changed. We moved from uncertainty and surface-level conversation to accountability.

The definition of accountability is simply being held accountable and responsible for our actions. You can't have honest accountability without complete authenticity. Accountability is the showing of self to others and making a concerted effort to grow. There is something inherently special about being able to admit you need help in an area and asking someone else to come alongside you. If I desire to be held accountable for my actions, I need to be honest with myself and the person I have asked to hold me accountable. I think there is a misconception when it comes to what healthy accountability is and what it looks like, so I will discuss the characteristics of both the healthy accountability giver and the healthy accountability asker.

Goals of the Healthy Accountability Giver (Butterflies): Being Open and Transparent and Seeking Accountability

You've been asked to do something that is a big deal; this person is counting on you to help them be responsible for their actions in a particular area of their life. As such, it is up to you to do your detective work to find out the reason behind what they are asking accountability for and how committed they are to taking steps toward growth and change. With my friend who also shared how she struggles with disordered eating, we discussed when our binge-eating episodes occurred, talked about why we think they happened, and tried to set a plan in place to stop that from happening in the future. Healthy accountability givers help you find out your why and assess how committed (how willing) you are to do what is needed (sometimes sacrifice) in order to meet your goal.

The nature of my goal related to food, not because I wanted to look better, weigh less, or restrict my calories. Sure, those things are desirable, but I knew my personal issue was deeper than just saying no to dessert. As I began working with my accountability partner, we pinpointed certain triggers (remember those?) related to my emotions that sparked a felt need to binge eat, and my brain had been wired to only look toward eating as a solution or release.

The emotions I determined I needed to address were loneliness, sadness, and worry. These hot-button emotional responses I felt potentially could send me into a spiral and derail any progress I had made.

The second goal of a healthy accountability giver is to understand and appreciate that growth is never linear. There will be slip-ups, there will be oopsies, but the important thing is helping the other person come up with their own conclusion about what lesson they've learned through the process. The goal is to strive for progress, not perfection. As we practice awareness, acceptance, and accountability, we are more than halfway there.

So my plan was to write in my journal, text my friend, or pray when I felt any of those emotional triggers start to bubble up. My ultimate goal was to feel the feelings and not try to push them under. I didn't do what I said I was going to do at first. Sometimes, I gave in, and sometimes, I willfully chose not to do what I said I was going to do. Then there were times I did have small victories. It is the small victories we have that keep us moving forward. As an accountability giver, we need to celebrate all victories, no matter how small.

What do we do when we mess up? What happens when we let our life circumstances derail what we set out to do? I've seen many people try to shame others into changing their behavior (mainly in the health and fitness industry). Some people think if you feel bad enough for what you did, you won't do it again. They suggest that shame is a strong motivator and that if you feel enough of it, you will do what it takes to stop it. In perpetuating this belief, they attempt to create conviction in you. They want you to feel bad for what you did or didn't do.

It is not our job to convict others; only God
has the power to do that.

It isn't up to us to try to make someone else feel convicted. Understanding that allows us to be free to fly and respond to others in love. It is acceptable to speak the truth in love, even if it is somewhat harsh, but know that your conversation should always be "seasoned with salt" (Col. 4:6) and grace.

> *Instead, speaking the truth in love, we will grow to become in every respect the mature body of him who is the head, that is, Christ.*
>
> —Eph. 4:15

> *Let your conversation be always full of grace, seasoned with salt, so that you may know how to answer everyone.*
>
> —Col. 4:6

Our goal is to provide *grace-filled accountability*. How we react and respond in a safe environment produces grace-filled accountability. We want to continue to be surrounded by people who foster our growth and authenticity. Grace-filled accountability assures us that it is okay to mess up because we are still loved. I wrote a letter to my dad, begging him to seek salvation in Jesus. I told him that even if he chose not to pursue a relationship with God, I would not love him any less. It was important for him to know that I love him unconditionally. I wanted him to know that my love isn't dependent on actions he decides to take or not take; it will always be there. His response to that letter was not loving. In fact, he did not handle it well at all. He was short, sarcastic, and rude. His harsh words cut deep, but that didn't stop me from sharing the love of Christ with him.

Sometimes, the reaction, even a negative one, is God planting a seed or even just preparing the soil. Healthy accountability often means setting appropriate boundaries while continuing to support the person in a way that doesn't hinder their growth. To hinder growth and potential in another is to do for them what they can do for themselves. What we don't often realize is that there is growth in the preparation and the struggle, especially when it involves the butterfly emerging from the cocoon, as we'll see in the story below.

The Story of the Butterfly

Once a little boy was playing outdoors and found a fascinating caterpillar. He carefully picked it up and took it home to show his mother. He asked his mother if he could keep it, and she said he could if he would take good care of it.

The little boy got a large jar from his mother and put in it plants for the caterpillar to eat and a stick for it to climb on. Every day he watched the caterpillar and brought it new plants to eat.

One day, the caterpillar climbed up the stick and started acting strangely. The boy worriedly called his mother who came and understood that the caterpillar was creating a cocoon. The mother explained to the boy how the caterpillar was going to go through a metamorphosis and become a butterfly.

The little boy was thrilled to hear about the changes his caterpillar would go through. He watched every day, waiting for the butterfly to emerge. One day it happened; a small hole appeared in the cocoon, and the butterfly started to struggle to come out.

At first the boy was excited, but soon he became concerned. The butterfly was struggling so hard to get out. It looked like it couldn't break free. It looked desperate. It looked like it was making no progress.

The boy was so concerned that he decided to help. He ran to get scissors and then walked back (because he had learned not to run with scissors). He snipped the cocoon to make the hole bigger, and the butterfly quickly emerged.

As the butterfly came out, the boy was surprised. It had a swollen body and small, shriveled wings. He continued to watch the butterfly, expecting that at any moment the wings would dry out, enlarge, and expand to support the swollen body. He knew that in time the body would shrink and the butterfly's wings would expand.

But neither happened.

The butterfly spent the rest of its life crawling around with a swollen body and shriveled wings.

It never was able to fly.

What the boy didn't realize was that the butterfly was *supposed to struggle. In fact, the butterfly's struggle to push its way through the tiny opening of the cocoon* would have pushed the fluid out of its body and into its wings.

Without the struggle, the butterfly would never, ever fly. The boy's good intentions hurt the butterfly.

—Author Unknown

So the struggle isn't necessarily only what we do once we are in the cocoon; the very process and steps it takes to get out of the cocoon are just as important for our spiritual growth. There needs to be a delicate balance between doing too much for someone and being disinterested and disengaged from helping them. In a grace-filled accountability relationship, we attempt to "spur one another on toward love and good deeds" (Heb. 10:24). That doesn't mean we do the work for them. It also doesn't mean we should tell them what to do. Accountability works not as an all-or-nothing agreement but as a relentless pursuit of becoming more like Christ. The truth is that we are all working toward something. We must understand that life will get in the way, but the most important thing is to get back on the wagon. Don't let someone fall away or drift away without checking on them.

As a small group leader and Bible study facilitator, I find it important to check in with people when they miss a week. I want them to know their absence doesn't go unnoticed and that they are an important member of the group. Group dynamics can be tricky, and sometimes people will stop doing something (even if they were super motivated at first) because they feel no one notices or even cares. The devil is looking to put every excuse in your head *not* to do something, so the more encouragement you can provide for someone (especially biblically based encouragement), the more it will drown out the voice of the enemy telling them they don't matter and shouldn't even try.

And let us consider how we may spur one another on toward love and good deeds, not giving up meeting together, as some are in the habit of doing, but encouraging one another—and all the more as you see the Day approaching.

—Heb. 10:24–25

There is a time and a place for biblical encouragement. Sometimes, people just need you to listen to where they are and what they are going through, especially during those hard, cocoon times. As an accountability partner, you don't have to have all the answers. All you need to do is show love to the other person. Love causes us to seek to encourage one another and offer support. There are enough people in this world who will tear you down, so why not focus on lifting each other up? Being able to provide the kind of accountability that fosters growth and change starts with having realistic expectations. Some activities or things that are part of your daily life already have their own built-in accountability.

In a Bible study, for example, there is usually a required reading or homework to do outside of class in preparation for the next week. I've talked to women who stopped attending Bible study because they were unable to do the homework. While we seek to hold others responsible for their actions, including taking steps toward spiritual growth, we don't hold it against them when they are unable to complete it, despite their good intentions.

I am happy that the ladies who attend my Bible study still decide to come even when they don't do their homework. They are very candid about not being able to complete the homework for class as we offer them grace and support. Being okay with them not getting their studies done isn't the same as excusing them from it. While I offer understanding, I also try to bring them back to their why and come up with ways to make it more manageable. At this point, we need to help the person remember why they set this goal in the first place and why it is important to them. It helps determine their personal immediate goal and the overall goal of every believer.

Forgetting what is behind and straining toward what is ahead, I press on toward the goal to win the prize for which God has called me heavenward in Christ Jesus.

—Phil. 3:13–14

Of course, just like with everything, there are some obstacles to overcome when you are helping someone stay accountable. If we are not careful, these can cause us to stumble or cause others to stumble, so they are better described as blind spots. These blind spots bring a butterfly back down and prevent them from flying and reaching their ultimate potential.

If Satan can't stop your growth,
he will try to stunt your growth.

Blind Spot #1 – Making Assumptions

I think we are all guilty of making assumptions about other people every now and again. It is human nature to judge others and hold them to a certain standard or expectation, but one way to avoid falling into this trap is to avoid assuming you know the reason behind the person's behavior.

I recently took on a friend as a coaching client. She also happens to be a fitness coach, so we somewhat trade our services. Early in our coaching relationship, we established her goals and what it would take to get her there, but the follow-through wasn't consistent. She would forget we had a session scheduled or completely ignore me when I tried to contact her. Because of her flakiness, I assumed that she wasn't getting value out of our agreement and didn't like coaching with me. Finally, we were able to connect, and she confided in me that she had been really struggling, and that was why she didn't reach out. Again, my assumption led me to believe it was me, but really it was her, and as her accountability partner, I let her down when I stopped checking in. My assumptions interfered with my being able to give proper, grace-filled accountability.

Blind Spot #2 – Making Excuses

We tend to think of the person who is supposed to be completing the action as the one who makes excuses or reasons for not doing it, but the person who is giving you accountability can also make excuses. The type of excuses can be related to the goal or related to the advice ("Sorry, I wasn't really listening" or "You've had a lot on your plate, so I didn't expect you to be able to do it"). While we offer forgiveness and understanding, we need to be careful not to make allowances for repeat behavior.

Blind Spot #3 – Making Comparisons

Far too often, we compare ourselves and our progress to others. It's simple. We can't compare our progress with others because everyone's journey looks different. It is detrimental to compare ourselves with others and tell them about it. Sure, we mean well when we tell the person that the other person working on their same goal was able to stick to it this past week—so why couldn't they? But statements like that are not usually motivating. Instead, they are embarrassing and even insulting.

The bottom line is this. We want to encourage and motivate the person, but we can't do the work for them since the lasting motivation to complete their goal must come from the Holy Spirit inside them. We can fan the flame, but they must have the spark inside themselves to begin with.

Goal of the Healthy Accountability Asker

> *Therefore, since we are surrounded by such a great cloud of witnesses, let us throw off everything that hinders and the sin that so easily entangles. And let us run with perseverance the race marked out for us.*
>
> —Heb. 12:1

Before we can set out to meet our goal, we need to fully understand our why. We need to ask ourselves some deeper questions to help investigate further regarding our reason for the goal, what makes it worthy of sacrificing, and why it is so important. What is your main motivation behind your action?

You want to read the Bible more. Great! So *why* is that important to you?

You want to exercise. *Why* is that important to you?

You want to save more money. *Why* is that important to you?

What is the implication of your actions now toward your life later? How will your life benefit if you read your Bible more? If you exercise more? If you save more money each month? There is always a future action dependent on your ability to reach your goal.

Examining your motivation behind your *why* helps you fully visualize the outcome. Fully engaging your senses in this visualization can make the dream feel more tangible. When you invest time into imagining what life would look like with the desired outcome, you have started what is known as self-actualization. Breaking down each line in Hebrews 12:1 will help explain this more.

Therefore, since we are surrounded by such a great cloud of witnesses.
This "cloud of witnesses" refers to your people. This is your community, your tribe, who is there to cheer you on as well as catch you when you fall. As the person asking for accountability, you should remind yourself that you are not doing this alone; you and your accountability partner are in this together (along with God).

Let us throw off everything that hinders and the sin that so easily entangles.
We know that it isn't up to us to fix ourselves, and we allow God to have His way in the area we are struggling with. Having the freedom to be authentic and transparent, we can list our triggers and decide to avoid them. Living from the place of freedom to be who God called us to be, we throw off everything that hinders and the sin that so easily entangles because true spiritual growth is an endless pursuit to understand the heart of the Father. The desire to be better causes us to do better.

And let us run with perseverance the race marked out for us.

Perseverance refers to determination and grit. That means that despite the obstacles we face, we never stop running. When we slip up, we don't stay there, but we do what we need to do to get back on track. Remember that every action moves you closer to God or away from Him. Our paths are already made, and it is up to us to keep moving forward in the right direction.

Every choice I make is either leading me down the path God has for me or leading me away from what God has for me. Think of your typical day. What do you do every day? Think of the many decisions you make each day, even the ones you make before 10:00 a.m. Why do you do what you do, and why do you choose one thing over another?

If we lack intention behind our choices,
it is harder to live out our purposes.

I am currently in a season of raising two young children, and my youngest doesn't sleep through the night. That means that on the rare occasion when I wake up before my little ones, I have two choices: I can get up and start my day, or I can turn back over and try to catch a few moments of precious sleep. Both of these decisions will affect the rest of my day, but there isn't necessarily a right or wrong answer. Even so, one has the potential to move me closer to the heart of the Father, and one could potentially move me away. If I am able to get up and have my quiet time before the chaos ensues, that choice will help keep me on the right track for the day. On the other hand, if I am able to take a few more minutes and get some sleep, there is no telling whether I would oversleep at that point or how I would feel after such a short stretch of sleep. (The most challenging thing about not getting enough sleep is waking up every 45 minutes to an hour, because when I get a solid four- to six-hour stretch, I feel like a new person.) If, however, I have a goal to complete a 15-minute quiet time per day, my motivation to reach my goal will affect my decision.

Therefore, a goal or a plan is important because otherwise we can easily make choices based on our feelings or incorrect thoughts fueled by false beliefs. If I want a cookie, I should be able to have a cookie. I know that one cookie isn't harmful, but a whole box of cookies might be. If I'm having a day when I'm upset or lonely, a cookie might look appealing to me, but sure enough, one cookie is a slippery slope for me, so I choose not to indulge.

We know that we are each created with a unique purpose for the glory of God. Even though we may not know exactly what that is, we do know when we aren't making the best choices related to our spiritual growth. That is when our outward actions need to reflect our internal hearts. Living like the transformed creatures we are is so important. What we think about is reflected in what we do. That includes actions and words. Examining our hearts and true motives for seeking a goal will show us where our true treasures lie.

For where your treasure is, there your heart will be also.

—Matt. 6:21

"I have the right to do anything," you say—but not everything is beneficial. "I have the right to do anything"—but I will not be mastered by anything.

—1 Cor. 6:12

A good man brings good things out of the good stored up in his heart, and an evil man brings evil things out of the evil stored up in his heart. For the mouth speaks what the heart is full of.

—Luke 6:45

The success of an accountability relationship can be measured in the area that we set our initial goal and how much it affects others around us. For example, as a child, I was never allowed to watch the cartoon *Rugrats* because my mom was convinced that I would start acting mean and bratty like Angelica. Even though I ignored this rule and watched the show, not thinking anything of it, I started to mirror her behavior. Just being immersed in her attitude, I was developing an attitude. That is also why being choosy when choosing our close friends is so important. They have an influence on us whether we like it or not. That is not to say that you should only have Christian friends or only hang out with Christians, because Jesus surrounded Himself will all types of people—robbers, tax collectors, and prostitutes, just to name a few. The caution here is to be careful who we let in our inner circle and who we allow to influence us.

We know that "bad company corrupts good character" (1 Cor. 15:33). We've talked about the importance of a supportive circle before, but think about it in terms of the people you hang around. Eventually, the way they talk or act will rub off on you.

Are you hanging around people who will encourage you and sharpen you, or are you hanging around people who are unwilling to let go of worldly comforts and have made peace with intentional sin? Do you think you are being pulled away from God by the company you are keeping?

> *As iron sharpens iron,*
> *so one person sharpens another.*
> —Prov. 27:17

> *Do not be misled: "Bad company corrupts good character."*
> —1 Cor. 15:33

I recently went back to my hometown for a wedding. I was around many people I didn't really know. There was a lot of cursing. I can't stand cursing; it actually usually causes me to wince or tense up when it's used in everyday life. However, I was around these people, and f-bombs were flying out left and right. It started to not upset me as much; I could hear what they were saying and became used to the curse words and colorful language they were using. Over time, maybe by the third straight day of being around these people, not only did I not mind the language they were using but I also caught myself speaking in a similar way more than once. It was so easy to drop a curse word every now and again because everyone was doing it; it seemed more awkward not to curse. The company we keep, or the people we are around, influences us for the better or for the worse, and it is a slow fade into these social sins.

On the flipside, I do have some very strong Christian friends whom I look to for spiritual wisdom and guidance. They are firmly rooted in the Lord, and many of our casual conversations are centered on what God is doing in our lives. How refreshing it is to be surrounded by other women who love Jesus.

Recognizing the type of friends we hang around who influence us represents just one of the many kinds of choices we have to make to guard our hearts and protect our spiritual growth. We need to take inventory of the good, or the fruit, that the choices we make are producing. The proverbial iron can only sharpen another piece of iron and cannot sharpen wool.

In our discussion on the importance of asking and receiving proper accountability for goals related to our overall growth and purpose, consider these verses:

> *Therefore encourage one another and build each other up, just as in fact you are doing. Now we ask you, brothers and sisters, to acknowledge those who work hard among you, who care for you in the Lord and who admonish you. Hold them in the highest regard in love because of their work. Live in peace with each other. And we urge you, brothers and sisters, warn those who are idle and disruptive, encourage the disheartened, help the weak, be patient with everyone. Make sure that nobody pays back wrong for wrong, but always strive to do what is good for each other and for everyone else.*
>
> —1 Thess. 5:11–15

Remembering the fruit of the Spirit, I challenge you to view each choice you make by the fruit it has the potential to bear. We know the Holy Spirit is not only in us but working inside us based on the fruit we produce. Let's examine what each fruit might look like in our everyday lives. Also keep in mind that we might not be able to see the growth in ourselves, and we might only be aware of the growth that is taking place in us because of another person who sees it and points it out.

> *But the fruit of the Spirit is love, joy, peace, forbearance, kindness, goodness, faithfulness, gentleness and self-control.*
>
> —Gal. 5:22–23

I'm not going to tell you what actions or behaviors display the fruit of the Spirit because they look different for everybody. Take a few minutes to do this exercise: List three actions, choices, or behaviors that display this fruit *in your own life*. These can be either things you are currently displaying or what you want to display. Remember that we don't all display the fruit of the Spirit in the same way, and we don't display them the way we think we do. As butterflies, we all are different and unique. No two journeys are alike.

I want to encourage you to never neglect speaking of the growth in another person. Sometimes, it is harder to keep trudging along a difficult path if you don't see progress. When you mention growth, you see and celebrate those victories, and it makes it a little easier to keep going. While moment-by-moment decisions can be what reflect the heart of God, how you respond to the world around you, especially circumstances in your life you can't control, speaks to your godly character. Taking what we've learned about the key attributes behind the butterfly mindset, we look at the importance of authenticity and action to be able to share our story and the gospel with others.

CHAPTER 9

The Purpose of the Butterfly

We help each other stay on track, and we help each other stay focused and remain in our lanes. The last key of the growth process—*action*—really doesn't come after accountability; it comes along with it. We are asking for accountability for actions, observable behaviors that measure our spiritual growth. So with accountability we can take action, but even with someone encouraging us and cheering us on, it can be hard to take that first step. Authenticity doesn't always precede accountability or action, but when it does, there is a key difference in not only the type of goals we set but also how we meet those goals.

I like to go to the gym, and I like to work out once I'm there. But in the time between my initial decision to go to the gym and my actual beginning to work out, I usually have a back-and-forth conversation with myself. I try to talk myself out of it and into it at least a dozen times.

You need to go do this; you'll feel better if you do.

Yeah, but I'm tired, and I don't feel like it.

It will feel good to get your body moving and blood pumping again.

But I just went the other day, so it's okay if I don't go today; no one is going to be mad.

When I do it, even though I don't feel like it at the time, I'm glad I did it. Sometimes, it takes more reassurance on my end, and other times, it takes more preparation and time. One thing that pushes me to follow through is my accountability partner.

> If she goes to the gym and tells me about it, I feel like if she can go, I can go, too.

> If she asks me if I'm going that day, I want to not only tell her my plan but be able to follow through with that plan.

Sometimes she talks me out of eating my weight in cookies or other sweet treats, while other times I'm the one to talk her off the ledge from stopping at the drive-thru on the way home from work. Either way, our friendship and accountability relationship, is rooted in trust, love, and understanding; I know she has my back just as much as I hope she knows I have hers.

Spiritually speaking, every action—even deciding whether to go to the gym or what types of food you eat—is either helping you become like Christ or pushing you away from Him. Keeping in mind that every choice and action has a spiritual consequence can also help you take that first step (remember my dilemma about sleeping in?).

Ready, set, go! It's time to take a step forward. You have your supports in place. You know what you need to look out for, and you know that you can't become all that God has for you without complete surrender. We have our safeguards in place; all systems are up and running and ready to go. We are butterflies understanding who we are in Christ and that we are called to share our stories with others.

Now it's time to M.O.V.E.

M – **M**ake the most of every opportunity

O – **O**vercome obstacles

V – **V**alue your emotions

E – **E**xpect refining moments, not defining moments

Make the Most of Every Opportunity

This might seem self-explanatory. Of course, we should be making the most of every opportunity, but what does that mean? Well, I can tell you what it does *not* mean. It does not mean saying yes to everything that comes your way. Instead, examine how those opportunities present themselves and in what area of your life those opportunities exist. Evaluate the pros and cons from an emotional, logical, and spiritual perspective. If an opportunity is going to take you away from your family, is it worth considering?

Your family is your first ministry. That includes your husband and your children. I know at times it can seem as though you are just a mom or just a wife, but God has selected you to be your husband's helpmate and the mother of your children. Take comfort knowing God has equipped you with everything you need to be successful for what He has given you. Opportunities don't necessarily mean you have to lead Bible studies or add activities or events to your calendar. Your next opportunity may be to just be still and take in each moment.

I nursed my daughter until she was about 10 months, and then she weaned herself and wasn't interested in nursing anymore. Just before she stopped nursing, she would only nurse at night, so I knew that the time for nursing my first child would soon come to an end. I then made sure to hold her and cherish those nighttime feedings. You never know when it will be your last time to do something, and when it is your last time, you can't get that time back. The action step you need to take may be to be intentional about your time and to make sure your priorities are in order. Just as God made everything beautiful in its time, so will He also reveal Himself in time.

Be still, and know that I am God.

—Ps. 46:10

He has made everything beautiful in its time.

—Eccles. 3:11

Overcome Obstacles

Inevitably, when you decide to take a step in faith, opposition will arise. Opposition can be in the form of the thoughts that go through your head or situations or circumstances that pop up and make it harder for you to do what you set out to do. By tackling the reasons we remain stuck in a particular habit, we can be confident to take a step forward, even if we are unsure where we're headed. That helps us evaluate whether we are living from a caterpillar or butterfly perspective.

Is it a good thing to always be comfortable? Can we get too cozy in our cocoon? Even after we become transformed, are we comfortable just sitting on our leaf and never desiring to fly? Is it always a good thing to be content with how things are? Do we ever reach a point where good enough is good enough, so we just stop? Once a butterfly becomes a butterfly, is it done?

Spiritual growth is a mindset to adapt to and strive for.

I'm certain that on this side of heaven, we will never be fully transformed into the image of Christ. That won't happen until we enter heaven. The pursuit of spiritual growth and transformation should not be thought of as an item to check off our to-do list. Instead, spiritual growth is a mindset to adapt to and strive for. In this, the main focus is progress, not perfection. It is common to not want to leave our comfort zones. We know that there is comfort in the familiar—even in the dysfunctional. That is largely due to the perceived control we have over our environment, which contributes to our complacency. The truth is that if we aspire to grow—to truly grow into who God has called us to be—we must take a step into the unknown. We must have faith that God not only will be there to catch us when we fall but that He has a plan for our lives. We need to trust Him. As the butterfly emerges from the cocoon, it must be willing to use the wings God has given it to fly.

"For I know the plans I have for you," declares the LORD,
"plans to prosper you and not to harm you, plans to give you
hope and a future."

—Jer. 29:11

Does knowing He has a good plan for us mean that the fear of the
unknown goes away? No. It does mean, however, that we trust in Him
because God already knows every unknown we face. Nothing we do
surprises Him or catches Him off guard. Scripture tells us that God not
only knows our actions before we execute them but also our words and
thoughts. That is both humbling and comforting.

Before a word is on my tongue you, LORD, know it completely.
—Ps. 139:4

Before I formed you in the womb I knew you,
before you were born I set you apart;
I appointed you as a prophet to the nations.
—Jer. 1:5

Because God knows what we are going to do or say beforehand,
we can be confident that we can choose what thoughts enter our heads
or what words we will speak. Words can be a slippery slope, though,
because the words you speak have the power to build up or tear down
another person. This, as you may recall, is where we also develop the
labels for ourselves that we live under—labels that can prevent us from
stepping into who God has called us to be.

The tongue has the power of life and death,
and those who love it will eat its fruit.
—Prov. 18:21

We choose our thoughts; we filter through the thoughts that are not
from God, and from those God-given thoughts we speak truth, love, and
hope to others. The Bible tells us that we have control over our thoughts.

Finally, brothers and sisters, whatever is true, whatever is noble, whatever is right, whatever is pure, whatever is lovely, whatever is admirable—if anything is excellent or praiseworthy—think about such things.

—Phil. 4:8

We demolish arguments and every pretension that sets itself up against the knowledge of God, and we take captive every thought to make it obedient to Christ.

—2 Cor. 10:5

I believe that every obstacle we face is an opportunity to learn and grow and show others what we've learned. We don't grow unless we step up and step out. In the hard times and even the times when we feel isolated in our cocoon, which is training and preparing us for what lies ahead, God is with us, and we will never face our battles alone.

So do not fear, for I am with you;
  do not be dismayed, for I am your God.
I will strengthen you and help you;
  I will uphold you with my righteous right hand.

—Isa. 41:10

Value Your Emotions

I know this seems somewhat counterintuitive to what I've been talking about. Don't follow your feelings, and don't follow your heart because it is deceitful. We should never act from an entirely emotional standpoint. Instead, we should appreciate these emotions when they come up as they might be trying to tell us something. It's like the fuel light in our cars. It's annoying when it turns on, but it is an important notification that if we don't refuel soon, we will run out of gas. Strong emotional responses are indicators that something is out of balance or out of whack. Never be afraid of strong emotions that you experience, and always do your best not to judge yourself for the emotions you are feeling. God created everything, including our up and down emotions, which means they have meaning and serve a purpose in our lives.

Think of your emotional responses as a broad spectrum with a lower end and a higher end. The intensity of your responses does *not* measure your level or spiritual growth (e.g., you are upset and don't lose your temper) but instead indicates a spiritual matter that might need to be addressed.

In the work I've done on myself and my crazy eating habits, I've learned to let myself feel the feelings as they come up. Instead of saying, "What is wrong with me?" or "How could I feel this way?" I've learned to view each emotion as a response and not an action.

Valuing your emotions as indicators of something deeper going on within you means you do not judge them or judge yourself for having them. This idea of not judging our emotions but letting them go comes from the practice of mindfulness, which is a great tool to use to stop looking at the next thing and instead become intentional and appreciate where you are on your journey. Growth doesn't happen when you reach your destination; it happens on the way to your destination. You can value your emotions as a way of showing you something deeper without letting them dictate your behavior. The best way to illustrate this is by giving you a real-world example:

Let's say that remind my husband that I signed up to attend a webinar, and I ask him if he could please be home by 6:00 p.m. to take care of our daughter, so I can give the webinar my full attention. He says he will do that. However, next day, the day of the webinar, he doesn't come home until after 6:00 p.m., so I have no choice but to juggle attending the webinar and taking care of our toddler until he shows up. I'm irritated, and I know why, but after I address this with him (he says he got caught at work), I still am very short with him. Even though I thought had I addressed this issue after further reflection, I see *why* I am still upset.

I view his not coming home in time as a sign of disrespect and not being supportive of my goals. You see, the webinar I attended was about casting a vision, and when my husband didn't keep his promise to be home at a certain time, I internalized this as an indication that he didn't care about what I was trying to do, and he didn't respect me or the goals I was trying to set. Here's the bottom line. He said, "I got tied up at work," but I heard, "I don't support your ministry." That's the tricky thing with perspective. Our false beliefs almost always threaten our identity.

While this example exemplifies how my awareness led to an action, it also shows the importance of not taking your emotional responses at face value. It is important to dig a little deeper into the reason for your emotional reactions.

The action I chose to take once I connected the dots of my skewed perception was that I apologized and told him I interpreted his actions differently than what he intended. What he said didn't match what I heard, and out of that, I reacted instead of responding. There is an important distinction between reacting and responding in situations.

- *Reacting* is purely emotional. Think road rage where you don't think about what you are doing; you just do it and deal with the consequences later.
- *Responding* is more logical and rational as you take a moment to evaluate the consequences of your words or actions.

Aim to respond, not react. Responding indicates thoughtful intent and careful understanding, while reacting represents an unrestrained, immediate event that is somewhat unpredictable.

Think about letting a pot of delicious soup on the stove simmer versus boil over. Which one would you prefer? Let's make it our personal mission to respond instead of react to the world around us. The butterfly will respond and not react, taking careful thought before flying to the next flower.

Expect Refining Moments, Not Defining Moments

Whether you react or respond to a situation favorably or unfavorably, you need to know that those times don't *define* you, but they can *refine* you. When you lose your temper with your spouse or children, it's not because "that's just how you are." We examine our actions under the microscope to determine whether our choices are moving us toward or away from our relationships with God. The good news is that God is a God of second, third, and even fourth chances, and if you respond poorly the first time, He will give you another opportunity to apply what you learned as a result of your reaction.

You may or may not have heard the caution to never pray for patience because God will give you many opportunities to practice patience in your everyday life. We are refined, sharpened, and tested, but the good news is that when we endure things, we come out stronger than before. That is why we enter the cocoon as caterpillars but leave as butterflies.

This third I will put into the fire;
I will refine them like silver
and test them like gold.
They will call on my name
and I will answer them;
I will say, "They are my people,"
and they will say, "The LORD is our God."

—Zech. 13:9

If you can manage to look at your circumstances in terms of what you can learn instead of what you don't know or can't see, you will be able to see God in every circumstance.

Food for Thought Questions:

- What would Jesus do?
- How are your actions today moving you toward the person God has created you to be?

- How does the law of cause and effect apply to refining and defining moments?
- How will understanding these two principles help you keep moving forward?
- If you are not moving, in essence you are standing still. The opposite of active is inactive.
- How are you being active in the Kingdom of God? In what ways might you still be inactive in the Kingdom?

Taking all these things into account, we are ready to M.O.V.E. forward and commit to an action. Action in this sense is deliberate and intentional, based on our known motives. See a problem, strategize a solution, and put a plan in place to achieve our goal. But what happens if we act *before* we think? Will we respond in a way that is surprising, especially after having gone through this process of growth and transformation?

CHAPTER 10

The Cycle Begins Again

In the case of not knowing why we did what we didn't want to do, we work backward. Every action we perform and every choice we make has an underlying reason behind it. I remember having made progress with my binge eating struggles and going to the grocery store, walking up and down the aisles looking for something to buy to take home, hoping that some food would pop out for me to buy and eat.

Nothing popped out, and nothing came to mind. I passed the cookie aisle, the candy aisle, and even the ice cream aisle to no avail. Maybe I should have given up, but the truth was I wanted to binge eat. I wasn't feeling bad; I wasn't experiencing any of my usual trigger emotions, yet I was trying to convince myself that I wanted to eat impulsively. So what did I do? I bought some cookie dough and ate it. I remember so clearly that I didn't even want it. I was forcing myself to eat it out of habit, I suppose. Our choices or actions do not always reflect our thoughts, so how do we explain this?

I do not understand what I do. For what I want to do I do not do, but what I hate I do. And if I do what I do not want to do, I agree that the law is good. As it is, it is no longer I myself who do it, but it is sin living in me. For I know that good itself does not dwell in me, that is, in my sinful nature. For I have the desire to do what is good, but I cannot carry it out. For I do not do the good I want to do, but the evil I do not want to do—this I keep on doing. Now if I do what I do not want to do, it is no longer I who do it, but it is sin living in me that does it.

—Rom. 7:15–20

Actions can be independent of conscious thought, so you can do something without thinking about it. Our brain operates on two systems. The first system is conscious thought. It is what we pay attention to, and it requires mental energy. The second system operates in the background. This is the brain's attempt to automate, create space, and save mental energy. Think of driving a car; at first you must be consciously aware of every little thing, but over time driving becomes more automatic. You can be driving on your street without really remembering how you got there. Our brain will always try to save energy by creating mental shortcuts. As a consequence, our learned responses take some time and effort to successfully override.

Routines and habits that we get accustomed to threaten to become what we focus on when we attempt to control every aspect of our lives.

My particular action of binge eating was more than just a slip or unusual moment. It was my body's attempt to gain control in a familiar environment. Remember, there is comfort in the familiar and even the dysfunctional. So the outcome of the behavior isn't always what's desired, but there is comfort in the habit and the routine. Here is another example.

I drink coffee. I don't drink coffee necessarily for the effect it gives me (honestly, I can't tell what effect it has on me). But the routine of sitting down in the morning with my coffee—not necessarily the coffee—is comforting. Routines and habits that we get accustomed to threaten to become what we focus on when we attempt to control every aspect of our lives.

The best way to combat this is by working backward. We try to become aware of the false beliefs before they lead to an unforeseen action or stay stuck in a bad habit. That means that it all comes back full circle. The cycle is ever-changing and continuously moving. That is the beauty of God's design; growth is a never-ending process, and it is a cycle of growth. God isn't finished with us yet. The importance of all the key principles is to see God move in our lives more clearly and have a greater appreciation of His work. The same goes for the butterfly stages. Each one has its own challenges, but it also has its rewards, and we can see God move on our behalf through each one.

> *He who began a good work in you will carry it on to completion until the day of Christ Jesus.*
>
> —Phil. 1:6

Awareness Leads to Acceptance Leads to Authenticity Leads to Accountability Leads to Action Leads Back to Awareness

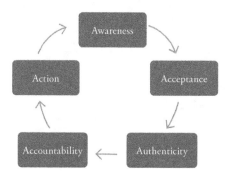

What exactly does this understanding of growth mean? It means that out of appreciation from our growth as a continuous cycle comes a greater dependence on God, which, dear friends, is exactly what we are created for. God is not a distant God. He didn't create the universe, make us, drop us onto earth, and leave us to fend for ourselves. He is ever-present and all around us. First and foremost, the Spirit of God lives within us, and His essence is scattered all throughout creation. For this reason, we are called into a relationship with Him, and one of the ways we gain that is by having a greater dependence on Him through the ordinary and the extraordinary.

> *And if the Spirit of him who raised Jesus from the dead is living in you, he who raised Christ from the dead will also give life to your mortal bodies because of his Spirit who lives in you.*
>
> —Rom. 8:11

I've alluded to the fact that you can be a caterpillar or a butterfly in different areas of your life; it's not all or nothing. So in the next few chapters, we will examine this idea by becoming aware of our weaknesses and learning how to depend on God to be our source of strength. The best approach to guide our goal-making efforts is what is known as a SMART goal.

CONCLUSION:
The Butterfly in Action

CHAPTER 11

The SMART Goal

So far, we've been doing what seems like an endless amount of self-reflection, practicing self-awareness. We've gone through each area of our lives, including our past and present, with a magnifying glass. We've been scouring every surface of ourselves for that slight imperfection that might signal a deeper problem. We've determined that a surface blemish or imperfection can be rooted in a deeper problem, and as we seek to remove this imperfection, we pluck it out intentionally, having found it only by using the magnifying glass and not some other tool.

What we don't always understand is that sometimes just looking through something isn't enough to be able to spot what we need to. It's like when you go through your kitchen junk drawer looking for batteries, tape, or a pair of scissors. You can't just open the drawer, look around, and then shut the drawer if you don't see it. If you really want to find what you opened the drawer to get, you need to move some stuff around. It's time to stop only wishing and visualizing; it's time to start doing. To make sure we don't miss anything, we must take our fine-tooth combs and go back over those areas we only previously skimmed with our eyes.

Friends, this is our call to action. We want to know what action we are supposed to take and what decision we should make. The struggle with inaction is the concern, pause, and eventual delay that comes between thinking and doing. One of the ways to avoid inaction or freezing up and not moving at all is to have a plan. It's not enough to just have a broad plan; you need a specific plan that will help keep you on track. This is the type of action plan that active butterflies refer to as helping guide and shape their thoughts and actions. This is how fellow butterflies encourage growth in one another through accountability. Let me introduce the power of the SMART goal.

Plans fail for lack of counsel,
    but with many advisers they succeed.
                                        —Prov. 15:22

A SMART goal is a specific, detailed strategy you come up with in order to help your goal become a reality. Here is the acrostic:

Specific
Measurable
Attainable
Relevant
Time-Specific

Specific

People look at *specific* in terms of goals all the time. Is your goal specific? If it isn't, it is going to be impossible to follow the other characteristics, including measurable. The most obvious example of a specific goal versus a non-specific goal is in terms of health.

It's not enough to just have a broad plan; you need a specific plan that will help keep you on track.

Health Goal:
    Non-specific goal: I want to eat healthily.
    Specific goal: I want to eat vegetables with every meal.

This an obvious example, so let's look at a less obvious one.

Spiritual Growth Goal:
    Non-specific goal: I want to have a closer relationship with God.
    Specific goal: I want to pray more.

First, we narrow our broader wants and desires to one specific point. While there are several different areas under the scope of healthy eating and spiritual growth, we choose one area to focus on. At this point, most people who talk about and use the SMART goal system will move on to the next part. But I caution anyone who uses the SMART goal system to come up with a detailed plan to give yourself plenty of time and space to determine what subarea to focus on. That is where the Wheel of Life tool may also come in handy; this tool is located in the "Resources" section of this book.

Questions to ask yourself when determining what subarea to focus your goal on:

- What is the single most important activity I need to add or eliminate that will help me achieve my goal?
- How challenging is it for me to commit to set a goal in a particular area?
- Have I prayed about what area I need to work on the most? (Prayer should be an integral part of your SMART goal-planning process.)

Remember, we are wired to want to reap the maximum benefit without having to put in a lot of work and effort. Just ask my students who do the bare minimum to get a passing grade or everyone who tries to lose weight by taking a pill or wearing a wrap. We want the reward without putting in the work. The activity you desire to add or subtract that will contribute to your overall goal may be somewhat challenging to complete, but it shouldn't be impossible. You need to find a balance between a challenging area to work on and something you see as more manageable.

What you decide to add to achieve your goal must be relatively easy to implement; that is, something that will require little to no additional effort. Adding a vegetable doesn't require a special shopping trip or much added time or expense, so maybe that's a good place to start.

The saying goes, "If you fail to plan, you plan to fail." While I don't like the word *fail*, I do understand the point that is being made. That is why it is so important to choose just one area and activity in that area; any more than that, and you will overwhelm yourself. If I tell myself I need to do all of the following things at once, I will get overwhelmed.

Eat more vegetables.

Do not drink soda.

Do not have dessert.

Make sure to track calories.

Drink only two cups of coffee per day instead of three or four.

If I don't know what to do, I'm not going to do it. So I encourage you to spend some time with God in prayer so He can reveal what area or activity in that area you will do or not do that will give you the outcome you desire. Small steps will always be easier than giant leaps. Remember that apple analogy in Chapter 2? Once you have figured out what action to focus on, you can move to the second step—making sure your action is measurable. We are only able to keep track of progress toward our goal if we know what progress and positive steps in the right direction look like.

Measurable

The science nerd in me is going to come out for a moment. When something is measurable, it means it is observable. Some constructs—

like love, for example—can't be measured directly. Instead, you must look for an action or a behavior that demonstrates that quality. *What kinds of behaviors do you believe demonstrate love?* We could say all types of things. We could say that hugging, kissing, or telling someone you love them can measure love. Then the question becomes this: Do all these behaviors measure love the same, or is there one that might reflect more love than the others? This concept goes back to the idea that love isn't an all-or-nothing action, so what observable action that you perform can measure a little or a lot of love? *How do we quantify these actions?*

If you are looking to measure love and you believe that counting hugs and kisses is a way to do that, then that is an example of how you will measure this. Here is the best question to ask yourself when you try to come up with a measurable goal: *Using the behavior you intend to measure, can you easily determine whether you met the goal for the week?*

Let's go back to the examples we gave earlier about health and spiritual growth.

Health: The action we want to add is to include a vegetable with every meal. That means your goal is to eat a vegetable with breakfast, lunch, and dinner—or three times per day.

Will you be able to tell whether you meet your goal each day? Would someone else on the outside looking in be able to observe and measure your behavior to determine whether you meet your daily goal?

Yes. While you could keep track of how many vegetables you eat each day, the best way may be to record when you eat a vegetable with your meal. For example, you could record that you had only two vegetables on Sunday and Thursday but had three each of the other days of the week. Keeping track or making an account of when you complete the desired action serves a dual purpose. It helps you keep track of your progress and serves as an additional motivator.

You're never too old for charts with stickers, and don't underestimate the satisfaction of crossing something off your to-do list. We are motivated toward things that matter to us. If you place a heavy importance on health and wellness, you will be more likely to do the necessary things in order to achieve your goal. The same thing goes for the importance you place on your spiritual growth.

Spiritual Growth: The action we want is to pray more. Okay. Observing and recording whether we are praying more is a good initial step, but we need to ask ourselves some additional questions to help us determine whether we are focusing on the intended behavior.

How many times a day do you pray now?

How many times a day do you desire to pray?

We need to establish a baseline of behavior and then use increments to increase our behavior. It might be unrealistic to say you want to pray five times per day if you currently do not pray at all. However, if you currently pray three times per day, then setting a goal of five times per day might not be too much of a stretch to achieve. It can be less about numbers and more about intention. Whatever you decide to look at as your checkpoint, it should be something that is possible for you to do. Setting an attainable goal will help set you up for success instead of making you feel like you are constantly behind or running on a hamster wheel.

Attainable

Here are the next questions to ask yourself when setting your goal: Is this goal attainable? Is it enough of a challenge but also something I can accomplish? If you have a goal that is too easy, then you risk staying in your comfort zone because you never have to push yourself. On the other hand, if you have a goal that seems unrealistic and unattainable, you run the risk of quitting before you ever get started.

> *But he said to me, "My grace is sufficient for you, for my power is made perfect in weakness." Therefore, I will boast all the more gladly about my weaknesses, so that Christ's power may rest on me.*
>
> —2 Cor. 12:9

I don't know many people who would use this verse when talking about setting a goal they feel they'll stick to. Most people prefer to highlight their strengths in terms of goal-setting.

I challenge you to set your goal not of your own strength but of Christ's strength and power within you. Set a goal that highlights your weaknesses, and watch God's power rest on you.

The truth is that we all have a baseline of actions and behaviors we perform throughout each day. So the easiest way to set a realistic and attainable goal that measures those behaviors is to add or subtract to our daily actions in small amounts.

If you want to run a 5K race and you've never run a day in your life, you aren't going to step outside and attempt to run a 5K right away. That's just asking for trouble. Instead, follow a plan to gradually add miles each day you train, and if you have never run before, start walking and jogging and then work your way up to running.

Setting a goal that is attainable allows you to keep in pursuit of the goal. You celebrate those small steps of accomplishments until you can look back and see how far you've come.

In this way, no goal is unattainable or unrealistic. Think about it. Ephesians tells us about what Christ is able to do for us and within us.

Now to him who is able to do immeasurably more than all we ask or imagine, according to his power that is at work within us.
—Eph. 3:20

The goals we set under the direction of Christ can't be limited or confined. In writing this book, I set a goal to write 30 minutes per day. What I ended up doing (not of my own power and will but of God's) was writing 1,000 words per day, and that was more than I had ever thought or imagined was possible, especially with my other commitments and responsibilities. It was the same when I needed to add more words. I thought I had said everything I needed in 20,000 words, but through God's guidance and direction, I was able to double that.

Remember, God shows up when we show up.

Then you will call on me and come and pray to me, and I will listen to you. You will seek me and find me when you seek me with all your heart.

—Jer. 29:12–13

God honors the time we set aside for Him. He honors our intentions as much as He honors our actions. That is because we are dedicated to Him, and that is demonstrated through our dependence on Him. We are called to be good stewards of what God has given us. When we are in a butterfly mindset (i.e., transformed), we understand that everything we do and everything we have does not belong to us; it belongs to the Lord.

Now, our God, we give you thanks,
    and praise your glorious name.

"But who am I, and who are my people, that we should be able to give as generously as this? Everything comes from you, and we have given you only what comes from your hand.

—1 Chron. 29:13–14

Each of you should use whatever gift you have received to serve others, as faithful stewards of God's grace in its various forms.

—1 Pet. 4:10

As part of our transformation, it is our responsibility to discover what our spiritual gifts look like and use them to help and serve others. I'm not going to go into a lot of detail about spiritual gifts, but I will say that if this interests you and you would like to read more about them and even take a quiz to help you determine what your gifts are, I recommend taking a look at www.giftstest.com. Our spiritual gifts also help guide the goals we should set. From the point of a specific, measurable, and attainable goal, we need to make sure our goal is related, or relevant, to our overall vision.

Relevant

This next point might seem self-explanatory, but it's important to take into consideration when writing a SMART goal. Is your step or goal relevant to your overall mission or vision for that particular area?

Health: We want to eat healthily, so we decide to set a goal of eating a vegetable with every meal. We need to ask ourselves this: Does this goal of eating more vegetables contribute to the overall goal of being healthy?

To determine whether your goal is relevant, we must think in terms of the future. We cast our vision to see how our desired outcome influences us physically, spiritually, and emotionally.

Not only does this help keep us motivated when we visualize how we will be different upon completion of the goal, but it also ensures that our goal and vision are related. For example, if I want to focus on being healthy, I won't set a goal to do laundry four times per week. The two aren't related (and besides, I hate doing laundry).

While I was studying research methods in college, I learned an analogy that explains the relationship between validity and reliability. Let's discuss these in further detail and how they relate to having a relevant goal.

Validity: How valid or correct is it? In terms of research methods, it is related to how well the activity you choose to observe demonstrates your construct. Think back to the love example. There isn't a way to measure love. Instead, we have to measure the behavior displayed by people who have love. Are you really measuring what you think you're measuring?

Reliability: This is related to how consistent your measure is. How likely are you to get the same results over and over again across different points in time? Thinking again of the love example, if you follow one couple and record the number of hugs they give each other each day, you would expect that to remain consistent each day.

You can have reliability without validity, but you cannot have validity without reliability. If I seek to determine how tall someone is by looking at the color of their eyes, I have a reliable measure (their eye color remains constant), but my measure is not valid because there is no relationship between the color of your eyes and your height.

So we want to put our effort in something that is going to matter and help us reach the overall goal, making sure that SMART goal is relevant and helps us get one step closer to where we want to be.

Spiritual growth: I've decided to pray more. I've decided to pray in the morning and at night, so I set my goal to help my spiritual growth based on an activity I can do that will get me closer to where I want to be. I would not set a goal of cleaning one room in the house each day because it is not relevant or related to my overall goal for spiritual growth.

When we are working through the first two steps, we most likely determine a specific measurable action that is relevant to the bigger picture. Now we take it one step further and make our goal time-specific, not just when I get around to it. The importance of a time-specific goal is that it helps us make a tangible plan so we can continue to take steps toward growth.

Time-Specific

I cannot express enough the importance of having a goal that is time-specific. To keep momentum going, you must set a time constraint for yourself. A time frame can be the amount of time you want to achieve your goal or the amount of time you want to be consistent in your actions.

You may have heard that 21 days of doing something repeatedly constitutes a habit, and once you make something a habit, it is harder to break. The caveat is that a habit must be attached to a meaning or value in order to stick. We can do something repeatedly, but we must be experiencing some reward (satisfaction) in response to the behavior.

Health: The satisfaction you are experiencing in response to the goal you set is that you are committed to eating vegetables. You also have learned some new delicious recipes, and your children are also eating vegetables with every meal (and not complaining).

Spiritual growth: The satisfaction you feel after you pray is unlike anything you have felt before. You feel connected to God in a whole new way, and you seem to have both a better day and a better night's sleep when you pray after waking and before you go to bed each night.

Just like when we gradually add or subtract to get to our desired level, we also start with a timeline. This timeline can be a random set amount of time or a time frame that is directly related to our goal.

When we see programs that promise we can go from our couch to running a 5K in three months, we know the time frame of three months (or 12 weeks) is put in place to motivate us until our desired end point (often the race we signed up for).

In our vegetable and prayer examples, I suggest trying it for a week and then reassessing the goal and adjusting, if necessary. We have to be willing to redefine, reevaluate, and sometimes throw out the first goal once we realize what we can be doing to see the results we desire and expect.

We need to be careful using the words *desire* and *expect*, however. I'll explain why and what words you may want to use instead.

Danger Words: Desire and Expect

I desire to do something.

I expect to do something.

Why are these words danger words?

We are not robots. We are not machines. You can't just plug in an algorithm and expect your desired result. There are outside factors that influence how well we actually put our plan into practice. One of those factors is related to mindset. Are we viewing our SMART goals as expectations or desires? How can thinking of our goals in this way keep us stuck?

If you desire to do something, it usually means you intend to work toward that desire. If you view your goal as a desire, you only have a simple dream or vision that you don't intend to put forth the effort to achieve. It will remain intangible and impossible since it is probably 10 years from now. From that perspective, you have handicapped yourself to not be able to reach your goal. You are caught up in wishful thinking. It is important at this point to go back and try to identify any false beliefs or triggers that are related to your desire. Are you still stuck in your caterpillar ways?

Expectations can keep us in bondage.

If you expect to do something, you are putting an overwhelming amount of pressure on yourself. Expectations can keep us in bondage. When we don't live up to our expectations, we can take drastic measures to meet our expectations. When we set expectations, we are still living under the false belief that we can completely control our circumstances. Setting unrealistic expectations does more harm than good. Having a healthy and realistic view of yourself is so important. Don't set expectations, and don't set desires. Set goals you can actualize and attain through the power of the Holy Spirit.

Here are the right words to use: *encouraged, motivated, inspired, focused, intentional. Intentional* is a great word to use in relation to your goals. It doesn't mean you intend to do something; it means you will be intentional to _____.

CHAPTER 12

Your Step-by-Step Guide to Becoming a Butterfly

I want to make this process as easy to follow and as understandable as possible. I am providing a step-by-step guide to understanding an awareness to action and how to take your initial goal and make it a SMART goal. This guide will also explain how changes in our thinking contribute to the caterpillar-to-butterfly transformation.

Step 1: Awareness: What from your past is skewing your perception? This step requires taking a thorough look at yourself to get the answer to what has created the false belief(s) you carry around with you. *This is the beginning, at the egg stage and caterpillar stage, where you realize something isn't quite right.*

Step 2: Acceptance: Can you accept who you are through the lens of being redeemed in Christ? We realize that all the junk we have thought about ourselves and how it altered our reality made us understand that we must accept Christ's ultimate sacrifice for us so we can hand Him our mess. And He will turn it into something that brings glory to Him. *This is the caterpillar who has made a decision to follow Christ, stop feeding on the things of this world, and start feasting on the Word of God.* This can also be applied to the cocoon stage, where you realize where you are and accept that there is a reason for the trial you are going through.

Step 3: Authenticity: Once we accept ourselves for how we are and who we are, we are ready to be our authentic selves in the appropriate setting. We ask ourselves what we are so afraid others will know about us. How can sharing our story help someone else? *This is evident in the cocoon stage where we are experiencing worry, fear, anxiety, pain, loss, and more.* In this stage, it is important to be authentic and transparent with those around you. Authenticity is also important in the butterfly stage as God uses our authenticity and transparency to help transform others.

Step 4: Accountability: Once we share our authentic selves with others, we are admittedly ready to discuss our struggles in order to be held responsible for our actions. We know God calls us higher each and every day and does not desire for us to remain stuck or stagnant. We also know that God wants us to be in community with others. Healthy community is imperative for our spiritual growth. Asking for accountability is challenging, but it starts with an understanding of a new standard. We aren't subject to be the way we are because we've always been that way; instead, we are called for greater things. Great accountability helps us live out our potential. *This happens in the last step when we've been changed into a butterfly.*

Step 5: Action: Sometimes, we need healthy accountability in order to feel comfortable enough to act. Many times, the baby steps we take are exactly what we need to feel the confidence to keep pressing into what action God is calling us to. The steps we take to better ourselves also can influence others to do the same. *As butterflies, the mindset is to continue to live out our purpose and encourage others to do the same.*

Step 6: SMART Goal: Taking action helps us have a plan in mind since we know that without a vision, people perish (Prov. 29:18). Although the Bible tells us that we can plan all we want, it reminds us that it is God who determines our steps (Prov. 16:9). Knowing where we are going is crucial in knowing who we are. Making a SMART goal is a strategy to actualize what you believe God is putting on your heart to grow you into a deeper relationship with Him. However, you should hold onto this plan loosely and never underestimate the power of God to blow your goals, your plans, or your ideas out of the water.

Specific	Is your goal detailed enough and based on a specific action?
Measurable	Can you observe the action to determine whether you met your goal?
Attainable	Is this something that is realistic to where you are, stretching you but not breaking you?
Relevant	How well does this goal relate to your bigger goals?
Time-Specific	What time limit binds this action to determine what, if any, changes need to be made?

In taking all these steps into consideration, the next logical question might be this: In what area of life should I set my goal? This is a great question, and when completing the Wheel of Life (located in the "Resources" section of this book), you will see how rating your satisfaction in a particular area is affected by your awareness of any false beliefs you carry or the triggers that threaten that belief.

Breaking down your satisfaction in the various areas according to the Wheel of Life might seem contradictory to what I mentioned— that every area surrendered to God is an area for spiritual growth. But think about the word *surrender*. As you go through each of the areas in the Wheel of Life, ask yourself this: Is that area of my life wholly surrendered to God?

If it is, how have you seen God move in that area?

If it isn't, what is stopping you from surrendering it, and can you surrender that area to God today?

Fully surrendering and fully trusting stem from a transformed mind through the power of Christ. This is the butterfly perspective.

*Fully surrendering and fully trusting stem
from a transformed mind through the power of Christ.
This is the butterfly perspective.*

Here are a few things to note about the Wheel of Life. It is a tool that many coaches use when helping clients find areas of their lives they want to improve. That is why the number you assign to each area (1–10) is so important. In each of the areas that you see a lower number than you would like, ask yourself this: What would it take to move from __ to 10?

The different areas or spokes of life can also be confusing, so I have provided an example for each area. There are distinct differences between all the areas, so make sure you evaluate yourself in each area with a critical eye.

Social stewardship, social life, memberships: a night out with friends

Spiritual life, your personal relationship with Jesus: quiet time

Physical stewardship, health, wellness: eating and exercising

Pace of life, work-life balance: number of commitments or responsibilities

Living space: physical space you live in

Another great exercise to do with the Wheel of Life is to have your significant other, a close family member, or friend complete it. It is interesting to get their take on your level of satisfaction in each area. It can also open your eyes to a specific area you need to work on that you weren't aware of before.

CHAPTER 13

Butterfly Declaration

On the pages of this book, I have laid out every step, every trick, every thought, every behavior, every choice I believe to be relevant when developing a closer relationship with God, understanding your purpose, and being completely transformed. I've shared a few examples of how my journey, my story, and my testimony have led me to write this book to help you achieve the growth you deserve in your friendships, marriages, and relationship with the Lord.

I want to leave you with a story, which involved one of my earliest coaching clients. This story is about how we identified her area of dissatisfaction using the Wheel of Life, worked through the five A's to spiritual growth, and saw her life ultimately changed forever. As I discuss her story, see if you can pick out the areas of thinking and behaving that were caterpillar-like versus butterfly-like.

> Hallie (name changed for confidentiality) was my first coaching client; in fact, she was my internship client. I'll never forget our first meeting. I was nervous and tried hard to hide it and maintain my professionalism. After she completed the Wheel of Life, she discussed all the areas and why she rated them the way she did. She decided that finances was the area where she needed my help.

But as we started talking more about finances and her ability to save and make enough money, the conversation started to go in a different direction, as it tends to do when led by the Holy Spirit. The topic of her spiritual life came up, and when I asked her a few questions about her daily time with God, it became obvious that she wasn't where she wanted to be but also didn't know how to change her mindset to make her quiet time happen.

When I told her I could help her remain committed to making her time with God a priority, I don't think she believed me. I told her I would provide her support, encouragement, and accountability to help her fall back in love with God. She cried when I said that, and I believe they were tears of excitement, relief, and anticipation. So we got started. We met weekly to discuss the week before—what was good, what wasn't good, and what she thought she needed to change.

When we met to evaluate her goals, we identified some obstacles that hindered her growth. The outward reasons for not getting her time in with God was that there wasn't enough time, and she was tired. What we both discovered through digging deeper (really becoming aware of false beliefs and false perceptions that had affected her for years) is that her ability to receive love and feel deserving of love and intimacy with God had been hindered by early childhood trauma and abuse. (This is a good rule of thumb. If you find yourself unable to complete your action step because you run out of time, it's time to look deeper into your underlying reason for procrastination.)

This huge revelation painted a much different picture than this one: I want to, but I just can't seem to make myself do it. Awareness of her false perception of herself and how she viewed God led her to be completely vulnerable and transparent with me. She started to accept herself and accept how much God loved her. We hear it all the time, that God loves us, but if someone feels undeserving of that love or carries fear or shame, they unknowingly build walls that make it harder to accept that truth. As she shared details of past abuse and addiction, I saw the thread of God's grace being woven into her story. Through her willingness to be authentic and share the hard stuff, healing and restoration took place, but it wasn't anything that I said or did. I simply invited God to move, and through her openness and vulnerability, He healed parts of her that I'm not even sure she had thought needed healing.

She ended our time with this note of encouragement: "Every area of my life is better because of you and your obedience to God's instruction."

Obedience to God isn't only mine to demonstrate; it is also yours. Listen to what God is trying to tell you about your life. Take a moment and try to fathom how much He loves you and desires a close and intimate relationship with you. Ponder what it means to surrender everything that does not serve you in the capacity you have to serve Him.

I implore you to take a step toward your spiritual growth. I realize that it is hard to unsee what you've already seen and unlearn what you already know, but don't look at it that way. The caterpillar isn't meant to stay a caterpillar; it is predestined to go into the cocoon and emerge as a butterfly.

Look at this as learning how to see clearly for the first time. Look at it not as unlearning or starting over but as discovering a revelation of the truth.

---

*Look at this as learning how to see clearly for the first
time. Look at it not as unlearning or starting over but as
discovering a revelation of the truth.*

I want to end by discussing a well-known story—actually two
stories—in the book of Mark. In both cases, Jesus heals blind men, but
as we look at both instances, note the differences between the two.
Jesus heals the first blind man:

> *They came to Bethsaida, and some people brought a blind
> man and begged Jesus to touch him. He took the blind man
> by the hand and led him outside the village. When he had
> spit on the man's eyes and put his hands on him, Jesus asked,
> "Do you see anything?"*
>
> *He looked up and said, "I see people; they look like trees
> walking around."*
>
> *Once more Jesus put his hands on the man's eyes. Then
> his eyes were opened, his sight was restored, and he saw
> everything clearly.*
>
> —Mark 8:22–25

Jesus heals the second blind man:

> *Then they came to Jericho. As Jesus and his disciples, together
> with a large crowd, were leaving the city, a blind man,
> Bartimaeus (which means "son of Timaeus"), was sitting by the
> roadside begging. When he heard that it was Jesus of Nazareth,
> he began to shout, "Jesus, Son of David, have mercy on me!"*
>
> *Many rebuked him and told him to be quiet, but he shouted
> all the more, "Son of David, have mercy on me!"*

Jesus stopped and said, "Call him."

So they called to the blind man, "Cheer up! On your feet! He's calling you." Throwing his cloak aside, he jumped to his feet and came to Jesus.

"What do you want me to do for you?" Jesus asked him.

The blind man said, "Rabbi, I want to see."

"Go," said Jesus, "your faith has healed you." Immediately he received his sight and followed Jesus along the road.

—Mark 10:46–52

Let's view some of the points in the first miracle:
- The people brought this man to Jesus.
- Jesus took the blind man by the hand and led him outside the village to heal his sight.
- He healed him in two steps: he spit on his eyes and put his hands over them.
- When asked if he saw anything, the man answered that he saw men walking like trees.
- Jesus put his hands over the man's eyes again and restored his sight.
- We don't know the blind man's name.

Let's view some of the points from the second miracle:
- Jesus heals Bartimaeus (we know the name of the man).
- Bartimaeus asks Jesus for healing.
- Against what others told him, he was persistent in calling Jesus over to heal him.
- The crowd changed their tune once Jesus spoke.
- Bartimaeus threw off his cloak and ran to Jesus.
- Jesus asked him what he would like Him to do.
- Jesus heals him, telling him that his faith has healed him.
- Jesus tells him to go his own way, but instead, Bartimaeus follows Him.

Perspective: Reality. For both men, their perspectives were their reality, and they didn't know any different. For Bart, he needed to realize and vocalize his weakness and greatest need so Jesus could restore his sight. For the first blind man, he needed to be honest about what he saw the first time.

Look where Jesus meets both men and heals them.

With a willing and receptive heart, Jesus will meet you right where you are, no matter where that is.

Once healed, Bartimaeus followed Jesus. The miracle Jesus performed preceded Bartimaeus' message. His message was of his faith making him well, and the story of the blind men with restored sight now became what they were to share with others. The best way to understand God's faithfulness is to experience it for yourself. But when we hear of stories about His faithfulness and goodness in other people's lives, it makes us hungry for that type of relationship. Hunger is a natural drive we have, and to satisfy that hunger, we go after a stronger relationship with God and His Word.

With a willing and receptive heart,
Jesus will meet you right where you are,
no matter where that is.

Your miracle, your growth, and your transformation become your story. It isn't something that happens to you; it is you. Your entire life is made up of decisions, choices, and behaviors that you choose every day.

Your miracle, your growth,
and your transformation become your story.
It isn't something that happens to you; it is you.

Food for Thought Questions:

- What do you notice that Jesus does differently in terms of restoring the sight of both men?
- How do both men respond?
- Does it matter that we only know the name of one man?
- Why does it take Jesus two shots to "get it right" the first time and then heals on the first try the second time?

Be like the blind men—both of them. Be able to speak what you need Jesus to do, and be able to be obedient to what Jesus asks of you. When you are given truth and the veil is lifted, allowing you to see clearly for the first time in a long time or maybe ever, run to Him. Pursue Him. Choose Him. Follow Him.

Do those things like your life depends on it—because it does.

Resources

Wheel of Life Exercise

how to

The Wheel of Life is a simple exercise to help you assess your satisfaction with the various areas in your life. For each of the sectors on the chart, rank yourself on a scale of 1 to 10. For example, if you are feeling great about your *Personal Development*, you might give yourself a 9. Then shade in nine-tenths of the *Personal Development* segment, starting from the inside out.

evaluation

The diagram below, when completed, can give you a picture of how your life currently matches up with how you want it to be. It can also give you greater clarity of what you want to work on with your coach. If you're not sure how to interpret the chart when you're finished, contact me. I'd love to help you work through it.

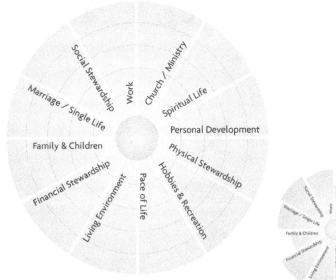

Wheel of Life Example: Relationship

S.M.A.R.T Goals

Goals are specific future targets that we are committed to becoming or accomplishing in an action-oriented, time-specific way.

S.M.A.R.T. goals are Specific, Measurable, Attainable, Relevant, and Time-specific. Use the definitions below as a guide for refining your goal:

Specific:
A goal is specific when you can describe it concretely to others.
Example: "I want to be wealthy" is not a specific goal—how much money is that? "I want to be a millionaire by the time I'm 40," or "I want to be able to retire at my current income when I'm 60" is specific.

Measurable:
You need to be able to tell when you've accomplished it.
Example: "I want to be a better businessperson" is not a measurable goal—how do I know when I am "better"? "I want to improve my business skills by completing a course in marketing this year" is a measurable goal.

Attainable:
It cannot be a pipe dream or something unrealizable.
Example: "I want to purchase 6 new rental properties this quarter" is probably unattainable if you are unemployed, have no collateral and no knowledge of the real estate industry.

Relevant:
A goal is relevant when it's important to you—when it references your values.
Example: "I want to be making all our payments on time by December" is a relevant goal for someone who is in financial difficulty and is highly motivated to make needed adjustments to reach their goal.

Time-specific:
Goals are not open-ended—they have dates attached.
Example: "I want to start a home for unwed mothers" is not time-specific; while "I want start a home for unwed mothers by five years from now (state a date)" is.

Scripture References for Each Chapter

Chapter 1

For God so loved the world that he gave his one and only Son, that whoever believes in him shall not perish but have eternal life. For God did not send his Son into the world to condemn the world, but to save the world through him.

—John 3:16–17

And you also were included in Christ when you heard the message of truth, the gospel of your salvation. When you believed, you were marked in him with a seal, the promised Holy Spirit, who is a deposit guaranteeing our inheritance until the redemption of those who are God's possession—to the praise of his glory.

—Eph. 1:13–14

Yet you brought me out of the womb;
*   you made me trust in you, even at my mother's breast.*
From birth I was cast on you;
*   from my mother's womb you have been my God.*

—Ps. 22:9–10

As for you, you were dead in your transgressions and sins, in which you used to live when you followed the ways of this world and of the ruler of the kingdom of the air, the spirit who is now at work in those who are disobedient. All of us also lived among them at one time, gratifying the cravings of our flesh and following its desires and thoughts. Like the rest, we were by nature deserving of wrath. But because of his great love for us, God, who is rich in mercy, made us alive with Christ even when we were dead in transgressions—it is by grace you have been saved.

—Eph. 2:1–5

Therefore, if anyone is in Christ, the new creation has come: The old has gone, the new is here!

—2 Cor. 5:17

As he neared Damascus on his journey, suddenly a light from heaven flashed around him.[4] *He fell to the ground and heard a voice say to him, "Saul, Saul, why do you persecute me?"*

"Who are you, Lord?" Saul asked.

"I am Jesus, whom you are persecuting," he replied. "Now get up and go into the city, and you will be told what you must do."

The men traveling with Saul stood there speechless; they heard the sound but did not see anyone. Saul got up from the ground, but when he opened his eyes, he could see nothing. So they led him by the hand into Damascus. For three days he was blind, and did not eat or drink anything.

In Damascus there was a disciple named Ananias. The Lord called to him in a vision, "Ananias!"

"Yes, Lord," he answered.

The Lord told him, "Go to the house of Judas on Straight Street and ask for a man from Tarsus named Saul, for he is praying. In a vision he has seen a man named Ananias come and place his hands on him to restore his sight."

"Lord," Ananias answered, "I have heard many reports about this man and all the harm he has done to your holy people in Jerusalem. And he has come here with authority from the chief priests to arrest all who call on your name."

But the Lord said to Ananias, "Go! This man is my chosen instrument to proclaim my name to the Gentiles and their kings and to the people of Israel. I will show him how much he must suffer for my name."

Then Ananias went to the house and entered it. Placing his hands on Saul, he said, "Brother Saul, the Lord—Jesus, who appeared to you on the road as you were coming here—has sent me so that you may see again and be filled with the Holy Spirit." Immediately, something like scales fell from Saul's eyes, and he could see again. He got up and was baptized, and after taking some food, he regained his strength.

—Acts 9:3–19

For the flesh desires what is contrary to the Spirit, and the Spirit what is contrary to the flesh. They are in conflict with each other, so that you are not to do whatever you want.

—Gal. 5:17

I do not understand what I do. For what I want to do I do not do, but what I hate I do.

—Rom. 7:15

Take delight in the LORD,
  and he will give you the desires of your heart.

—Ps. 37:4

The heart is deceitful above all things
  and beyond cure.
  Who can understand it?

—Jer. 17:9

Many are the plans in a person's heart,
  but it is the LORD's purpose that prevails.

—Prov. 19:21

Search me, God, and know my heart;
  test me and know my anxious thoughts.
See if there is any offensive way in me,
  and lead me in the way everlasting.

—Ps. 139:23–24

I have come that they may have life, and have it to the full.

—John 10:10

My prayer is not that you take them out of the world but that you protect them from the evil one. They are not of the world, even as I am not of it. Sanctify them by the truth; your word is truth. As you sent me into the world, I have sent them into the world.

—John 17:15–18

When the teachers of the law who were Pharisees saw him eating with these sinners and tax collectors, they asked his disciples, "Why does He eat with tax collectors and sinners?"

On hearing this, Jesus said to them, "It is not the healthy who need a doctor, but the sick. I have not come to call the righteous, but sinners."

—Mark 2:16–17

But thanks be to God that, though you used to be slaves to sin, you have come to obey from your heart the pattern of teaching that has now claimed your allegiance. You have been set free from sin and have become slaves to righteousness.

—Rom. 6:17–18

Do not conform to the pattern of this world, but be transformed by the renewing of your mind. Then you will be able to test and approve what God's will is—his good, pleasing and perfect will.

—Rom. 12:2

There is no fear in love. But perfect love drives out fear, because fear has to do with punishment. The one who fears is not made perfect in love.

—1 John 4:18

For I am convinced that neither death nor life, neither angels nor demons, neither the present nor the future, nor any powers, neither height nor depth, nor anything else in all creation, will be able to separate us from the love of God that is in Christ Jesus our Lord.

—Rom. 8:38–39

Chapter 2

*Do nothing out of selfish ambition or vain conceit. Rather,
in humility value others above yourselves, not looking to your
own interests but each of you to the interests of the others.*

—Phil. 2:3–4

*But the fruit of the Spirit is love, joy, peace, forbearance,
kindness, goodness, faithfulness, gentleness and self-control.
Against such things there is no law.*

—Gal. 5:22–23

Chapter 3

*When the woman saw that the fruit of the tree was good for
food and pleasing to the eye, and also desirable for gaining
wisdom, she took some and ate it. She also gave some to her
husband, who was with her, and he ate it. Then the eyes
of both of them were opened, and they realized they were
naked; so they sewed fig leaves together and made coverings
for themselves.*

—Gen. 3:6–7

I can do everything through Christ, who gives me strength.

—Phil. 4:13 NLT

Chapter 4

As for you, you were dead in your transgressions and sins, in which you used to live when you followed the ways of this world and of the ruler of the kingdom of the air, the spirit who is now at work in those who are disobedient. All of us also lived among them at one time, gratifying the cravings of our flesh and following its desires and thoughts. Like the rest, we were by nature deserving of wrath. But because of his great love for us, God, who is rich in mercy, made us alive with Christ even when we were dead in transgressions— it is by grace you have been saved. And God raised us up with Christ and seated us with him in the heavenly realms in Christ Jesus, in order that in the coming ages he might show the incomparable riches of his grace, expressed in his kindness to us in Christ Jesus. For it is by grace you have been saved, through faith—and this is not from yourselves, it is the gift of God—not by works, so that no one can boast. For we are God's handiwork, created in Christ Jesus to do good works, which God prepared in advance for us to do.

—Eph. 2:1–10

For all have sinned and fall short of the glory of God.

—Rom. 3:23

All of us have become like one who is unclean,
and all our righteous acts are like filthy rags;
we all shrivel up like a leaf,
and like the wind our sins sweep us away.

—Isa. 64:6

But he said to me, "My grace is sufficient for you, for my power is made perfect in weakness." Therefore, I will boast all the more gladly about my weaknesses, so that Christ's power may rest on me.

—2 Cor. 12:9

Chapter 5

Yet you, LORD, are our Father.
  We are the clay, you are the potter;
  we are all the work of your hand.

—Isa. 64:8

For all have sinned and fall short of the glory of God.

—Rom. 3:23

As for you, you were dead in your transgressions and sins, in which you used to live when you followed the ways of this world and of the ruler of the kingdom of the air, the spirit who is now at work in those who are disobedient. All of us also lived among them at one time, gratifying the cravings of our flesh and following its desires and thoughts. Like the rest, we were by nature deserving of wrath. But because of his great love for us, God, who is rich in mercy, made us alive with Christ even when we were dead in transgressions— it is by grace you have been saved. And God raised us up with Christ and seated us with him in the heavenly realms in Christ Jesus, in order that in the coming ages he might show the incomparable riches of his grace, expressed in his kindness to us in Christ Jesus. For it is by grace you have been saved, through faith—and this is not from yourselves, it is the gift of God—not by works, so that no one can boast. For we are God's handiwork, created in Christ Jesus to do good works, which God prepared in advance for us to do.

—Eph. 2:1–10

Chapter 6

I am not saying this because I am in need, for I have learned to be content whatever the circumstances. I know what it is to be in need, and I know what it is to have plenty. I have learned the secret of being content in any and every situation, whether fed or hungry, whether living in plenty or in want.

—Phil. 4:11–12

Give thanks in all circumstances; for this is God's will for you in Christ Jesus.

—1 Thess. 5:18

Do not be anxious about anything, but in every situation, by prayer and petition, with thanksgiving, present your requests to God. And the peace of God, which transcends all understanding, will guard your hearts and your minds in Christ Jesus.

—Phil. 4:6–7

Chapter 7

The light shines in the darkness, and the darkness has not overcome it.

—John 1:5

Carry each other's burdens, and in this way you will fulfill the law of Christ.

—Gal. 6:2

And we all, who with unveiled faces contemplate the Lord's glory, are being transformed into his image with ever-increasing glory, which comes from the Lord, who is the Spirit.

—2 Cor. 3:18

Therefore go and make disciples of all nations, baptizing them in the name of the Father and of the Son and of the Holy Spirit, and teaching them to obey everything I have commanded you. And surely I am with you always, to the very end of the age.

—Matt. 28:19–20

Therefore each of you must put off falsehood and speak truthfully to your neighbor, for we are all members of one body.

—Eph. 4:25

I have told you these things, so that in me you may have peace. In this world you will have trouble. But take heart! I have overcome the world.

—John 16:33

The secret things belong to the LORD our God, but the things revealed belong to us and to our children forever, that we may follow all the words of this law.

—Deut. 29:29

Chapter 8

Therefore confess your sins to each other and pray for each other so that you may be healed. The prayer of a righteous person is powerful and effective.

—James 5:16

Instead, speaking the truth in love, we will grow to become in every respect the mature body of him who is the head, that is, Christ.

—Eph. 4:15

Let your conversation be always full of grace, seasoned with salt, so that you may know how to answer everyone.

—Col. 4:6

And let us consider how we may spur one another on toward love and good deeds, not giving up meeting together, as some are in the habit of doing, but encouraging one another— and all the more as you see the Day approaching.

—Heb. 10:24–25

Forgetting what is behind and straining toward what is ahead, I press on toward the goal to win the prize for which God has called me heavenward in Christ Jesus.

—Phil. 3:13–14

Therefore, since we are surrounded by such a great cloud of witnesses, let us throw off everything that hinders and the sin that so easily entangles. And let us run with perseverance the race marked out for us.

—Heb. 12:1

For where your treasure is, there your heart will be also.

—Matt. 6:21

"I have the right to do anything," you say—but not everything is beneficial. "I have the right to do anything"—but I will not be mastered by anything.

—1 Cor. 6:12

A good man brings good things out of the good stored up in his heart, and an evil man brings evil things out of the evil stored up in his heart. For the mouth speaks what the heart is full of.

—Luke 6:45

As iron sharpens iron,
*   so one person sharpens another.*

—Prov. 27:17

Do not be misled: "Bad company corrupts good character."

—1 Cor. 15:33

Therefore encourage one another and build each other up, just as in fact you are doing.

Now we ask you, brothers and sisters, to acknowledge those who work hard among you, who care for you in the Lord and who admonish you. Hold them in the highest regard in love because of their work. Live in peace with each other. And we urge you, brothers and sisters, warn those who are idle and disruptive, encourage the disheartened, help the weak, be patient with everyone. Make sure that nobody pays back wrong for wrong, but always strive to do what is good for each other and for everyone else.

—1 Thess. 5:11–15

But the fruit of the Spirit is love, joy, peace, forbearance, kindness, goodness, faithfulness, gentleness and self-control. Against such things there is no law.

—Gal. 5:22–23

Chapter 9

Be still, and know that I am God.

—Ps. 46:10

He has made everything beautiful in its time.

—Eccles. 3:11

"For I know the plans I have for you," declares the LORD, "plans to prosper you and not to harm you, plans to give you hope and a future."

—Jer. 29:11

*Before a word is on my tongue
you, LORD, know it completely.*

—Ps. 139:4

*Before I formed you in the womb I knew you,
before you were born I set you apart;
I appointed you as a prophet to the nations.*

—Jer. 1:5

*The tongue has the power of life and death,
and those who love it will eat its fruit.*

—Prov. 18:21

Finally, brothers and sisters, whatever is true, whatever is noble, whatever is right, whatever is pure, whatever is lovely, whatever is admirable—if anything is excellent or praiseworthy—think about such things.

—Phil. 4:8

We demolish arguments and every pretension that sets itself up against the knowledge of God, and we take captive every thought to make it obedient to Christ.

—2 Cor. 10:5

So do not fear, for I am with you;
*   do not be dismayed, for I am your God.*
I will strengthen you and help you;
*   I will uphold you with my righteous right hand.*

—Isa. 41:10

This third I will put into the fire;
*   I will refine them like silver*
*   and test them like gold.*
They will call on my name
*   and I will answer them;*
I will say, "They are my people,"
*   and they will say, "The LORD is our God."*

—Zech. 13:9

Chapter 10

I do not understand what I do. For what I want to do I do not do, but what I hate I do. And if I do what I do not want to do, I agree that the law is good. As it is, it is no longer I myself who do it, but it is sin living in me. For I know that good itself does not dwell in me, that is, in my sinful nature. For I have the desire to do what is good, but I cannot carry it out. For I do not do the good I want to do, but the evil I do not want to do—this I keep on doing. Now if I do what I do not want to do, it is no longer I who do it, but it is sin living in me that does it.

—Rom. 7:15–20

He who began a good work in you will carry it on to completion until the day of Christ Jesus.

—Phil. 1:6

And if the Spirit of him who raised Jesus from the dead is living in you, he who raised Christ from the dead will also give life to your mortal bodies because of his Spirit who lives in you.

—Rom. 8:11

Chapter 11

*Plans fail for lack of counsel,
but with many advisers they succeed.*

—Prov. 15:22

But he said to me, "My grace is sufficient for you, for my power is made perfect in weakness." Therefore, I will boast all the more gladly about my weaknesses, so that Christ's power may rest on me.

—2 Cor. 12:9

Now to him who is able to do immeasurably more than all we ask or imagine, according to his power that is at work within us.

—Eph. 3:20

Then you will call on me and come and pray to me, and I will listen to you. You will seek me and find me when you seek me with all your heart.

—Jer. 29:12–13

Now, our God, we give you thanks, and praise your glorious name.

"But who am I, and who are my people, that we should be able to give as generously as this? Everything comes from you, and we have given you only what comes from your hand.

—1 Chron. 29:13–14

Each of you should use whatever gift you have received to serve others, as faithful stewards of God's grace in its various forms.

—1 Pet. 4:10

Chapter 12

Where there is no revelation, people cast off restraint;
but blessed is the one who heeds wisdom's instruction.

—Prov. 29:18

In their hearts humans plan their course,
but the LORD establishes their steps.

—Prov. 16:9

Chapter 13

They came to Bethsaida, and some people brought a blind
man and begged Jesus to touch him. He took the blind man
by the hand and led him outside the village. When he had
spit on the man's eyes and put his hands on him, Jesus asked,
"Do you see anything?"

He looked up and said, "I see people; they look like trees
walking around."

Once more Jesus put his hands on the man's eyes. Then
his eyes were opened, his sight was restored, and he saw
everything clearly.

—Mark 8:22–25

Then they came to Jericho. As Jesus and his disciples, together with a large crowd, were leaving the city, a blind man, Bartimaeus (which means "son of Timaeus"), was sitting by the roadside begging. When he heard that it was Jesus of Nazareth, he began to shout, "Jesus, Son of David, have mercy on me!"

Many rebuked him and told him to be quiet, but he shouted all the more, "Son of David, have mercy on me!"

Jesus stopped and said, "Call him."

So they called to the blind man, "Cheer up! On your feet! He's calling you." Throwing his cloak aside, he jumped to his feet and came to Jesus.

"What do you want me to do for you?" Jesus asked him.

The blind man said, "Rabbi, I want to see."

"Go," said Jesus, "your faith has healed you." Immediately he received his sight and followed Jesus along the road.

—Mark 10:46–52

Acknowledgments

I would like to thank the following people (in no particular order) who helped make this book possible.

Terry, thank you for always encouraging me to write and write well. Your friendship is invaluable to me, and this book would not have been possible without you.

Hillary-Beth, thank you for being that well-trained, second set of eyes this book needed to make everything streamlined and consistent. You truly captured my voice and tone and gave me the push I needed to take it in the "butterfly" direction.

The team at Lucid Books, thank you for seeing the potential in my book and believing in me to help bring the vision and message God gave me to fruition.

Chou, Elizabeth, and Jane, I am so glad our paths crossed how and when they did. I can't express how thankful I am for your support and your kind words, always.

Thank you to my family and friends who have been there every step of the way, encouraging me to keep writing this book. A special thank you to my Grandma Jane who is and always has been one of my biggest cheerleaders when it comes to my writing and speaking.

Lastly (and most importantly), thank you to God for sending Jesus Christ as my Lord and Savior. Thank You for rescuing me from the pit I was in and transforming my heart and mind. Thank You for the freedom I have in You and that You put these words in my heart to share with others.

CPSIA information can be obtained
at www.ICGtesting.com
Printed in the USA
BVHW091345170920
588981BV00013B/142